PRAISE FOR
CHASING GRACE

Sanya Richards-Ross has represented Team USA so well for her entire career. But she was born in Jamaica, and I can connect to the winner's spirit that we share. I'm proud of everything Sanya has accomplished, including the writing of *Chasing Grace*. Through her vulnerability in sharing some of her most personal stories of victory and defeat, triumph and tribulation, I once again see her strength. Big up yuhself, Sanya!

> **USAIN BOLT,** the world's fastest man, eight-time
> Olympic gold medalist, eleven-time World Champion,
> and four-time Laureus World Sportsman of the Year

Chasing Grace is an excellent read for anyone who is searching for ways to be encouraged and motivated to never give up on pursuing the dream. Sanya Richards-Ross, the five-time Olympic medalist, has illustrated throughout her career patience, perseverance, and perspective on what it takes to become a champion on and off the field with God's grace. *Chasing Grace* is the script for a manual that can help guide anyone wanting to be the best. Once you start reading, you will find it difficult to stop turning the pages in the anticipation of wanting more.

> **JACKIE JOYNER-KERSEE,** the greatest
> female athlete of the twentieth century

I will always say that I am eternally grateful to the game of football—for what it gave me and what it taught me. Through my sport, I learned to reach out to my family, teammates, and friends. It's a humbling moment when you realize you have the opportunity to share lessons learned and can support and encourage others to live the life of their dreams. I see that same sense of wonderment and responsibility in Sanya Richards-Ross on every page of her competitive memoir, *Chasing Grace*. More than a story about achievement and victory, Sanya's book delivers as a journey of discovery. It is honest and heartfelt, and I believe she openly examines her life's work in the pursuit of helping others live their dreams.

MICHAEL STRAHAN, entrepreneur, broadcaster, author, Pro Football Hall of Famer, and Super Bowl champion

Chasing Grace is not only the story of a young girl who followed her dreams and became an Olympic champion, but also a collection of valuable lessons that were learned along the way. Sanya Richards-Ross has written a wonderful book for those who want to be inspired and uplifted while learning how to successfully handle all the challenges we inevitably face in life.

LAILA ALI, world champion boxer, fitness and wellness expert, and television personality

Sanya Richards-Ross embodies what I consider to be a true American hero. Her ability to overcome obstacles and stay focused on her mission to be not just the best runner in the world but a world-class woman stirs me, and it will challenge and encourage all who read *Chasing Grace*. I so respect Sanya's journey and recommend her book to anyone looking to be inspired!

DARA TORRES, five-time Olympic
swimmer and twelve-time medalist

When I was a young athlete, my coaches used to explain what I should aspire to be, and Sanya Richards-Ross was always the standard. Powerful, graceful, caring; physically, mentally, and morally sound. You had to wonder how she came to be. Thankfully we don't anymore. It's a pleasure to finally read her operating manual.

ASHTON EATON, two-time Olympic decathlon
gold medalist and world record holder in both
the decathlon and indoor heptathlon events

In a world that often defines public achievement as success, Sanya Richards-Ross reveals in *Chasing Grace* that her greatest feat in life was not on a track for the world to see, but rather in her soul where God would serve as the ultimate coach. She now shares wisdom from the deep reservoir of her pains, joys, trials, and triumphs that will inspire us all to pursue the grace race with confidence, trust, optimism, and unshaken faith.

SARAH JAKES ROBERTS, author
and copastor of One Church LA

Chasing Grace is a remarkable story of a young woman who stayed the course to achieve her dreams. Like most success stories, Sanya faced many challenges that not only prepared her for Olympic Gold but prepared her for the real race of life. I commend her on having the courage to share her toughest moments, and I know her truth will inspire many.

ANGELA SIMMONS, fashion designer,
TV personality, and entrepreneur

Sanya Richards-Ross is one of the world's greatest athletes, but her success isn't just God-given. She took great talent and made it the best it could be by learning from others, working hard, and leaning on her family and her faith. She has always been about far more than athletic achievement. She has been an advocate and role model and has always taken a global view of her life and career. *Chasing Grace* provides a look at how she was able to overcome and succeed, both on and off the track.

MAX SIEGEL, CEO, USA Track & Field

Sanya Richards-Ross is the definition of a champion on and off the track. Her focus, ambition, and passion were evident dating back to our time at the University of Texas. *Chasing Grace* is an incredibly inspiring story of how she used her God-given abilities to win gold while ultimately finding her true purpose. I'm proud of the woman she has become and her bravery in sharing her story.

VINCE YOUNG, professional football player,
entrepreneur, and philanthropist

Chasing Grace embodies the determination needed to fulfill our lifelong dreams. Sanya Richards-Ross has done us all a favor by uniquely sharing her life stories to motivate, inspire, and empower individuals who read it. The 400-meter race is a great metaphor for life. It's an enduring race. This book is filled with life lessons that will enable the reader to progress from just being ordinary to becoming a true champion on and off the track of life. Grace—unmerited favor of God.

COREY WEBSTER, nine-season NFL cornerback
and two-time Super Bowl champion

Chasing Grace is an empowering story of walking in grace and purpose. Sanya Richards-Ross has passion and courage etched in every step throughout her career so far. This is how you do it.

ESTELLE, Grammy Award–winning
artist, actress, and producer

Chasing Grace doesn't just give you a look behind the scenes; it invites you into some of Sanya Richards-Ross's most personal moments. Moments fans often don't consider. Sanya's transparency is courageous and beautiful. Her words are eloquent, and the lessons shared are priceless.

LAURYN WILLIAMS, four-time Olympian
and first American woman to medal in both
the Summer and Winter Olympic Games

Chasing Grace gives the reader a glimpse into the mind-set of a rare athlete, Sanya Richards-Ross, who has the holy trinity of skills: the athletic ability to perform and win at the highest level, the poise to deliver a flawless live interview after, and the savvy to know how to build a successful brand from it.

ATO BOLDON, four-time Olympic medalist and
lead track and field analyst for NBC Sports

CHASING GRACE

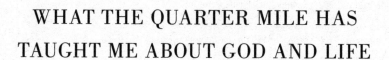

WHAT THE QUARTER MILE HAS
TAUGHT ME ABOUT GOD AND LIFE

SANYA RICHARDS-ROSS

ZONDERVAN®

ZONDERVAN

Chasing Grace
Copyright © 2017 by Sanya Richards-Ross

Requests for information should be addressed to:
Zondervan, *3900 Sparks Dr. SE, Grand Rapids, Michigan 49546*

ISBN 978-0-310-34940-2 (hardcover)

ISBN 978-0-310-35144-3 (international trade paper edition)

ISBN 978-0-310-35047-7 (audio)

ISBN 978-0-310-35017-0 (ebook)

Scripture quotations are taken from The Holy Bible, New International Version®, NIV®. Copyright © 1973, 1978, 1984, 2011 by Biblica, Inc.® Used by permission of Zondervan. All rights reserved worldwide. www.Zondervan.com. The "NIV" and "New International Version" are trademarks registered in the United States Patent and Trademark Office by Biblica, Inc.®

Any Internet addresses (websites, blogs, etc.) and telephone numbers in this book are offered as a resource. They are not intended in any way to be or imply an endorsement by Zondervan, nor does Zondervan vouch for the content of these sites and numbers for the life of this book.

Cover design: Curt Diepenhorst
Cover photography: Erick Robinson
Interior design: Kait Lamphere
Interior imagery: PhotoDisc

First printing April 2017 / Printed in the United States of America

To Coach Hart—

I am eternally grateful our paths crossed,
as your dedication to being the very best
at what you do aligned perfectly
with making my dreams a reality.
The golden moments we've shared on the track
pale in comparison to the memories we've made
and the life lessons you've taught me.
Thank you for the 4 P's!
They made me
the best 400-meter runner in U.S. history
and gave me a road map
to navigate through life with God.

CONTENTS

POISE: Commit to the Finish

PREFACE

The track has always been my safe haven. My sanctuary, my place of peace. I've always said I didn't choose the quarter mile, but it chose me.

Over time, I learned to love the race.

One full lap around the track—and my favorite part is the last 100 meters off the final curve. I feel free. I feel liberated.

Then, in an instant, a heartbeat, the freedom can turn to panic. When you sense the other bodies charging around you, and you are not sure if you're in a position to win, strategy is overtaken by intense desire.

Be first.

If you have to dive, fall, or hurl your body across the finish line, you'll do whatever it takes. It's an instinct that's within you.

But after making it through the tape, you have to wait. And you wait in faith.

When I won the Olympic gold medal at the 2012 London Olympics, I wasn't 100 percent sure I crossed the finish line first. In the few seconds between the end of the race and the announcement of the winner, I wanted to will my name to the top of the scoreboard, but I could only clasp my hands in prayer and believe all my hard work would be rewarded.

The photo finish showed I won comfortably, by a stride's length, but in the race's final moments, I still felt the need to dip my left shoulder and stretch my neck out over the line. Even to this day, when I see my right arm punching through the air, I don't know whether it's in celebration or a last-second reach to grab victory.

As most people equate success with having more, my quest was always for less. For as long as I can remember, life has been measured in seconds. The fewer, the better. I've been running track since I was seven—basically a life's worth of conditioning to run a 400-meter race in fifty seconds, hopefully forty-nine or, even better, forty-eight. Instinctively, my greatest source of validation was being the quickest to the finish line.

When I first stepped on the track to represent my Jamaican elementary school, Vaz Prep, I heard my parents, family, classmates, and friends cheering for me.

"Sanya a champion! Sanya a champion!" everyone called out. I won, and my name was in the headlines the next day in our local newspaper, *The Gleaner*.

I felt special. I was a champion. For more than two decades after that, I ran in circles around the track, chasing that same feeling.

It took a long time to realize I was of more value than a gold medal or a record-setting lap. For so long, I was just Sanya Richards the athlete, and I hung my head when I didn't run well.

My existence was all about my performance. Each loss came with a feeling of unhealthy and unwanted shame. Running, I had to figure out, is just what I do; it's not who I am.

Since I started to compete at the age of seven, my losses were measured against the hope of greatness. Champions measure themselves against other champions. Winning was simply confirmation that I belonged among the league of extraordinary athletes.

In retrospect, I believe my wins on the track sometimes led to losses in the race of life. From elementary school in Jamaica to the Olympics in China, physical, mental, and emotional confrontations have tested my character, my faith, and my resolve.

It has always been my desire to live a life transparent enough to allow others to learn from my mistakes. I want you to see me as I am. Bear witness to strength and weakness, highs and lows, goodness and sinfulness—my complete journey.

On that warm August night in London, I lunged my body forward, not completely sure of where it would land. I only had my faith.

Sometimes we need those moments—times when we are forced to be still and wait for the photo finish. I believe life is nothing more than a collection of photo finishes shot through the lens of God's camera.

For every exhilarating high like I experienced in 2012, there have been just as many—if not more—excruciating lows. I couldn't always understand how I could lose after I had trained so hard and competed with such focus. Eventually, I began to see that my losses were as significant as my wins. Every lesson I learned didn't just make me a better runner; each running experience molded me into a stronger person. I could finally look back and see the beauty of God's timing. And now I can look forward and trust His plan.

My journey carried me beyond the track. Through this book, I hope my stories will help you see your own experiences through God's lens as a life captured in a perfect photo finish.

THE 4 P'S: PUSH, PACE, POSITION, POISE

My Strategy to Running the Race with Grace

M uscles are my memory, and every memory a muscle. Years ago when I started training with my coach, Clyde Hart, he divided the quarter-mile race into four phases. Coach Hart called them the 4 P's: push, pace, position, and poise.

I work on each of the four phases in practice to ensure that when it comes time to race, my body responds, as my mind instinctively shifts from one phase to the next.

As I've gotten older, I still see the genius in Coach Hart's strategy. In some way or another, in some part of my life or another, I'm either pushing, pacing, positioning, or remaining poised.

I hope you can apply these strategies and learn how to run your best race—to live your best life.

PUSH: Chase Your Dream

The push part of the race takes intense focus. As you crouch over the track, feet staggered in the starting blocks, fingertips bracing your body over the start line, hips raised in the set position, the mind prepares to go from "0 to 100."

And that's how it happens. Zero to breaking a school zone's speed limit in a few strides. You push into the race with all your might. Sprinting is a power event, and with the technology of tracks today, the more you push into them, the more you get in return. The force from my feet actually allows the track to launch me forward into the next step.

Life, too, gives back what you put into it. Every day, you have the opportunity to push yourself to a higher gear or achieve a goal. Whether it's taking a full course load in college, making time to exercise, or devoting extra focus to a special project, you are propelling forward on a mission.

Believe that your persistence will be rewarded. You may not be able to see it or immediately feel it, but life honors that drive.

PACE: Create Your Rhythm

You get out of the blocks strong, coming through the first 100 meters of the race at nearly maximum speed. But it's not possible to maintain that speed throughout the entire quarter-mile race. The body cannot push that hard for that long.

At 100 meters, you have to throttle back and let the energy supplies refill with a little more oxygen. Your stride stretches out underneath the body and finds a smooth tempo. Arms and legs work together with the lungs to sustain the energy and strength necessary to shift to another gear and kick coming down the home stretch.

Runners need to find a rhythm they can settle into.

Everyone needs an awareness of what they can handle. The push phase sets you up to chase down your dreams, but pacing allows you to maintain your push for the long haul. Rhythm and routine set you up for greatness.

Evaluate what your mind and body can maintain. Make sure your priorities don't cause your spirit to burn out. Check in with your Creator so that your vision aligns with His purpose for you. Keep your pace in line with God's. No need to run ahead of Him.

POSITION: Go with Courage

When you're racing the 400, you don't start to really compete until the 200-meter mark. As you begin to work the final turn, now is the first time you even consider where your competition is and how the race will be won.

Prepare the body to throttle back to full speed. It's a snap-quick decision.

Decide. Then go for it.

It takes courage to execute the race plan. Coach Hart always said, "Most people will relax into the curve, but this is your advantage. This is where you have to start your kick. If you don't start your work here, you will lose seconds, and you won't be able to make them up.

Taking your position requires faith, discipline, and determination.

Where am I going? How badly do I want it? Will I stick to my plan when facing struggle, pain, fear, and doubt?

Evaluate all of these factors as you decide what you want out of life and what is required to get there.

POISE: Commit to the Finish

The final 100 meters of the race test your mind even more than your muscle. Remember to stay poised, because if you panic and lose your head, you're not going to win, even if the other phases are executed perfectly.

At this point in the race, you feel fatigue. It's only natural. Sometimes runners lose their form and start to flail. Losing your form is just like stopping or even going backward. Just hold your course. Don't let the mind convince the body it's failing, and distract you from winning the prize.

Hold on to your faith. Believe you did all the right things, and it's going to pay off. By this point, all the hard work is done. You just have to hold on and trust the process. Regardless of the outcome, be grateful and proud of your results.

PRAY: The Silent, Constant, Invisible P

Prayer is an essential element of *every* phase, and it does deserve practice. Every journey's beginning, middle, and end is richer and sweeter when shared with God.

When you pray, you ask God to intervene, and then submit to His will. Through gratitude and admission, you ask Him to take away your burdens, and by your faithfulness, trust Him to do it.

Prayer frees you from worry, doubt, and fear.

Prayer fills you with hope and reminds you of your greater purpose. Not to win races or make more money, not to become a CEO or a president, but in all things, serve and give glory to God.

Life on this earth, as I learned through running the 400, tests your mind, body, and spirit. And the most important thing you can do at every point is *pray without ceasing*. Sometimes you may struggle to know what to pray for or even how to pray, but the key is consistent communication. Open your heart, and let the Holy Spirit work through you. He knows all and sees all.

PUSH

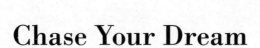

Chase Your Dream

Chapter 1

CHAMPION GIRL

Realizing Your Talent

*For we are God's handiwork, created in
Christ Jesus to do good works, which God
prepared in advance for us to do.*

EPHESIANS 2:10

I'm the only one awake in my house. It's still dark outside, maybe five or six in the morning, and I tiptoe around the bedroom, being careful not to wake my sleeping sister, Shari, as I quietly assemble my outfit.

Socks match my tank top. Tank top matches my hair tie, which also matches my wristband. I like to match. Show up. Dress up. "Look like you came to win," Mom said as she labored over my braids the night before.

I'm ready to go. I'm nine years old. Somebody has to get up and drive me.

"Baby, guh back to bed," Mom tells me from her pillow. "It's not time yet."

"I want to go now."

We didn't race until later that afternoon. I had all day to get ready. But I looked forward to running like it was Christmas morning.

Born in Kingston, Jamaica, where track and field is the country's prized pastime, I had no choice but to fall in love with the sport. Surrounded by murals and statues of track and field icons Merlene Ottey, Donald Quarrie, and Herb McKenley, I more readily knew their names and stories than I did of our prime minister. I wanted to be just like them. I wanted *my* picture on the wall.

To me, there was no other option than to run track. It started in elementary school. Every day after classes at Vaz Prep, we had practice on our school track. Well, it was just dirt and grass. There was no rubber surface or really even a track. Our coaches spray-painted the field with white lines so it resembled a track, but to me it was everything. I couldn't wait to get there each day.

It was exciting to realize joy and passion for something I really loved, to experience being good at something, to discover a God-given talent. I even thought the tedious drills that marked the beginning of every practice were fun. Before we could start running, we marched in place, our arms shifting as perfect ninety-degree levers, and then we'd do A-skips and B-skips. Those movements were an integral part of our development, and throughout my career, I'd never start a training session or line up to race without warming up with the exact same drills in the exact same order.

I did everything full bore, unafraid of what might go wrong. If I was hanging from the monkey bars, I'd try to swing too. As a result, I'd often fall and hurt myself. But I don't remember my youth as one of scrapes or bruises. I just kept moving, running toward whatever was next.

The Prep Champs are contested every year, determining the country's best youth runners. Tens of thousands of people fill the national stadium in Kingston, Jamaica's capital, to watch kids ages six to eleven run around a track. Imagine a carnival inside a track meet. Legions of school fans gathered in packs in the bleachers, waving flags, filling the thick, muggy air with drumbeats and rehearsed chants. At school in the days leading up to the meet, we'd practice, usually riffing on whatever reggae song was popular at the moment.

"Vaz Prep a champion! Vaz Prep a champion!" I can hear it to this day.

I first competed there when I was seven. The enormity of the meet, the energy, the competition, had adrenaline charging up and down my body. I was anxious, but mostly just excited to race—and to win.

Jamaicans are passionate in their following of track and field. In Jamaica, winning is prized. It's celebrated. Losing is an embarrassment. You're either first, or you're last. There's no in between. Since I won the very first race I ever entered at seven years old, the taste for winning was established early and quickly. Like an addiction. I wanted more. And I was happy to do the hard work to keep on winning.

I was fortunate enough to attend Vaz Prep, a high-quality school with a competitive curriculum that also afforded me national-caliber coaches. They set the team up for success by instilling mechanics at a young age and allowed us to practice block starts, even though we weren't yet using them in races.

By the time I competed in my third Prep Champs as a nine-year-old, anticipation was already building. My name and picture had appeared in the newspaper. People knew who I was and expected me to win, because that's what I did. I had never lost a race.

Wolmers, a neighboring elementary school, was our biggest rival, and the competition in the stands was already heated.

Schools occupied their own sections and baited each other with dueling chants, Jamaican style.

"She caan beat our girls dis year," they'd say. The legion of blue and gold, the colors of Vaz Prep, proudly claimed, "Sanya was di best last year, and she's di best again dis year."

A Vaz Prep chorus provided my walk-out music.

"Sanya a champion! Sanya a champion!"

It was raucous as usual, and in that moment, I felt invincible.

Our coaches were so methodical with their teaching, our technique so polished, that they encouraged us to get a little flashy with our starts. Not all the kids did that. Maybe it was just a way to gain an early edge on our opponents, but at the biggest meet of my young career, it nearly backfired. Actually, it *did* backfire.

We practiced our starts to stand straight (on your mark), go down and touch (set), and then rush off the line with the gun. This race, the girl on my left was already down before I set, and she shifted her position. It threw off my concentration. Instead of going down and getting in my ready position, I rocked back a little. I leaned back just as the gun fired to start the race.

Everyone else surged into their sprints. I stumbled backward. The sense of panic that washed over me awakens me even now. The realization jerks me to life.

"Sanya a champion!"

You're going to lose. I *can't* lose.

I had lost so much ground already, and in a 60-meter race, there isn't much time for misfires. By the time I straightened up and bolted off the line, I had given up several yard lengths.

It was the fastest I had ever run, an all-out, crazy, furious pedaling to convert panic into adrenaline. My mind and body were almost numb. The shouts and support of the crowd went silent, and I hurled along in a bubble. All I could see and feel were my lane and the finish line so many yards in front of me.

Run. Catch them. Keep running. Getting closer. Run. Move. Arms, Sanya, use your arms. Be strong. Ten yards to go. Almost there. Catch her. There's the line. Another two steps. Reach. Grab the line. Get through the line.

No. It's over. Did I lose?

I looked up to Dad, in his usual spot above the line, and I couldn't read his face. No one knew who won, but whoever did had won by an eyelash. It was close, a photo finish, and I had to run one of my best races just to make it close. With 10 yards still to go, there was daylight between me and the rest of the girls.

But then and there, all I could do was hold back tears.

"Sanya a champion! Sanya a champion!"

I blew it. I just knew it.

One of the longtime race officials who ushered runners on and off the track picked me up and hugged me as the group waited for the race results to be revealed. "Great job. Beautiful race," he told me. The tears were streaming down my cheeks by now. "I think I lost," I told him.

"No, you won."

"Are you sure?"

"Yes, you won!"

A warm sense of relief came over me. The painful stiffness of worry released from my body. I found my family for victory hugs, and Dad beamed.

"That's one of the best races I've ever seen, dahling," he said. "I did not believe it was possible. How did you get your shoulder in front?"

Blue-and-gold fans were in hysterics. "Sanya a champion! Sanya a champion!"

Everything else is faded. It's just a haze, almost like I blacked out and moved around the rest of the day on instinct. Never before had my body or mind been asked to shift so intensely. From a confident walk to the start line to a crazed dash to the finish. From the panic of failure to the reward of victory. Was I happy that I pulled off this amazing come-from-behind win—or that I was freed from the shame of losing in a blunder?

The funny thing is, I had already won a race earlier that day. I won the 150 meters. But this race was it. The 60 meters determines the fastest girl. And that was me.

As the meet concluded, my family had packed up and was getting ready to walk to the parking lot. I yanked on Dad's arm. I was stalling. They were preparing the field area for award presentations, and every year, they named a Champion Girl. If your performance is dominant enough by winning multiple races and relays, you get that distinction. And this year, I thought I had a chance. I wanted that trophy.

We were still in the bleachers, and the voice came through the speaker.

"The Champion Girl in Class Two . . . is Sanya Richards."

Dad was so proud. He picked me up, lifted me over the fence, and placed me on the track so I could accept the award. To be recognized by everyone, not just for winning races, but as the best in my age group—I was elated, and so was my family.

From then on, every trophy I could get, I went for it.

PUSH

When you finally realize your gifts and talents, joy and satisfaction come as you walk in your purpose. That's undeniable. God has uniquely prepared you for something special, and once you find your calling, run toward your passion.

Even when I fell backward, I still won the race. God ordains outcomes, and He divinely crafts us to find success. I knew early on that whatever God was to do through me was to begin on the track. You begin your push phase when you look to God to reveal your talent. By pursuing your talent, you respond to and experience God in special ways.

Chapter 2

A STAR IS BORN

Manifesting Your Talent

*The man who had received five bags of
gold went at once and put his money to
work and gained five bags more.*

MATTHEW 25:16

You can never accuse my father, Archie Richards, of not having a vision—or a plan to accomplish it. Once I was announced Champion Girl, my dad picked up a program and flipped through the race results and records. He noticed that my previous times in the youngest class were faster than the times of the boys the same age and the times of the girls a year or two older than me.

He didn't tell me until a few years later, but Dad realized I had a special talent then and there.

My mom, Sharon, isn't much into the numbers. Dad says she wasn't impressed by his fancy time-comparison chart. She's the diplomat of our family, making sure everyone stays even-keeled, but she believed in what he thought was possible. Everybody bought in.

Dad, Mom, and Shari were my first entourage. Competition begins before you ever set your feet in the blocks and brace for the gun. Racers size each other up out of instinct. Track is as pure as it gets—me against you—but I always felt strengthened by the collective will of my family. Walking into track meets, with the three of them around me, I felt invincible. We all knew what we came to do: line up and win.

Dad was our flag bearer. He led the way and set the tone. He decided early on that being able to review races on film would be essential to my development, so he bought a video camera and made sure to record all my races. That meant he had to have the perfect view, perched right above the finish line, regardless of the row and seat number printed on his ticket. He's a slight man, fit and fast, but far be it from any burly security guard to tell him he couldn't sit where he needed to be in order to capture the race on video. He would ignore stern instructions or bully his way if he needed to. He never intended to stay for the entire track meet, but he had to be in position and capture my race. No one could stop him. That countenance, paired with his inspirational words and constant encouragement, made me feel like I could win a race running backward.

Mom and Shari evened me out. I could always count on Mom to be polite and graceful, and to greet everyone with a quiet smile. She kept me calm.

"Be easy, Sanya. Don't get crazy, Sanya. Just win the race."

Shari was my backbone, reminding me of my hard work and preparation, confirming that I was a winner. And honestly, before every race, it's her voice that would start me as much as the gun. Silence envelops a crouched sprinter. Still and quiet, the entire stadium holds its breath.

"On your mark."

"Set."

Pistol pop.

"LET'S GO, SANYA!"

That's my Shari, using anything she could muster, her loudest voice, to reach down from the stands, lift me out of the blocks, and push me out around the track. I watch recordings of my professional races now, nationally broadcasted meets, and I hear Shari.

My family was my rock, and their support was crucial throughout our move to America.

Mom already had family living in the United States. Her sister had relocated from Jamaica to the Fort Lauderdale area in Florida. Though my education in Jamaica was top-notch, Mom knew scholarship opportunities were more readily available to American universities if I were to attend a high school in America. It took some convincing, though, especially Dad, before our family made the decision to move to Florida. But our new home was only an hour-and-a-half trip back to Jamaica, and the notion that I could compete for a scholarship—academically or athletically—and not have to pay for a college education eventually convinced Dad.

I was twelve when we officially made the leap and committed to a new path and new home in America. The transition wasn't easy, but it helped having family already in the Fort Lauderdale area. I'll never forget my first day of middle school. In Jamaica, we wore uniforms, but in my new school, we could wear outfits of our choosing. I planned for a week. I tried on everything in my closet before settling on a denim dress with white Chuck Taylors.

When I arrived to Pines Middle School for the first time, I was excited, anxious, and nervous, but some of that went away when I immediately got a compliment from one of my new classmates on my sneakers.

Thank You, God! Things were going to be great. I had nothing to worry about.

Then the teacher walked in to the first period class, and I stood. It was customary in Jamaica to stand when your teacher walked in and collectively say, "Good morning." I was so embarrassed when no one else did, and the kids looked at me like I was some foreigner standing there all alone in the class. I quickly sat back down and avoided eye contact. It was instantly clear I was no longer in Jamaica, and this was my first real indication that things were going to be different.

I was so used to being a leader—always voted class captain or prefect (what we called it in Jamaica)—but I now needed to learn that the best leaders first embrace the power that comes as a follower.

Grateful to see a familiar face, I shared the story with Shari at lunch. She almost cried laughing. Shari was somehow clever enough to wait patiently in her seat and avoid the embarrassment I endured. Shari and I were best friends, and our bond intensified, because early on, we really just had each other. We shared a bedroom in the small apartment our family lived in before settling into our permanent home. No matter what school we attended, Shari and I knew we'd have at least one friend, because we always had a friend in each other. I always went to the school cafeteria to check on Shari during her lunchtime, even if I had to make up a new reason every day to leave class. It was important to me that she was OK, that she had friends and was having a good day.

Mom's sister, my aunt Maureen, helped us research possible locations for our family's new home. She was a big part of guiding our transition to South Florida and made the biggest investment in my life by leading me to Christ. She was a faithful church-goer, a staple at what was then Caribbean Baptist Church (now ChristWay Baptist Church), and she would take us every Thursday for choir practice and Sunday for the worship service. I admired her passion and the quiet peace that defined her character. Even at age twelve, I knew there was something special about her that I wanted to emulate. I accepted Jesus as my Savior when I was thirteen. I was baptized and started living my life for Christ.

Aunt Maureen was also the one who identified the perfect spot for my continuing growth as a student and competitor. St. Thomas Aquinas started as a small, private Catholic school in 1936 and is now a campus covering almost thirty acres in urban Fort Lauderdale, offering students college preparatory courses in state-of-the-art classrooms and laboratories. The athletics facilities are pristine, like that of a small college, and provide the training grounds for an esteemed prep sports program. The Raiders have won more than a hundred state championships, and I'm proud to say that I donned the blue-and-gold while helping the girls' track team to four straight titles during my years there from 1998 to 2002.

The top-notch facilities weren't the biggest difference between athletics in Jamaica and America. Mostly, to me, it was the culture. In Jamaica, if you're in second place, you're the first loser. There's no way around it. I was more than a little taken aback when I competed at my first meet in America. One of my teammates was far back in the pack as she came around the turn and went down the home stretch in front of the bleachers, hustling toward the finish line. People clapped furiously and shouted support.

"Come on. Let's go. You got this."

What in the world? I thought. *She's behind. She's losing.*

It took me a little while to unlearn what was instilled in me in Jamaica, where there was no such thing as a participation ribbon. I had to learn to understand that sometimes you can be satisfied with giving your best effort and leaving it all on the track—no matter the outcome.

As a young Jamaican, I was also used to living in a community where most of the people looked just like me. Most of the students I went to school with and the individuals I interacted with were black.

St. Thomas Aquinas was a majority-white private school. Now I was in the minority.

I've heard many people say they don't see color, and it usually makes me skeptical, but I can honestly say at thirteen, one of the youngest kids entering the ninth grade, I never really felt like I was any different. I always loved people and went out of my way to make friends. Not just the people on the track team, but everybody.

If you were in my class, in the cafeteria, or even in the parking garage when I pulled up, I wanted to get to know you. It was fair to say I was among the popular girls at school and experienced sustained success on the track and in the classroom. Add a 4.0

GPA, and I had struck the perfect balance as a well-rounded student-athlete. Or at least *I* thought so.

Before the summer of my senior year, I attended the junior Olympics with one of my favorite teammates. I shared with her my new crush and how I hoped we would start dating during our senior year. He was the most popular guy in the school and the football team captain. Gregarious, handsome, and funny—all the girls liked him.

As I walked the hallways for the first day of my senior year, I saw my teammate, the one I had confided in, holding my crush's hand. My chest tightened, and my breathing quickened. I was in utter shock. *How could this be? When did this happen? Why didn't she tell me?* I was heartbroken. I was completely blindsided.

The dynamic of my intimate circle of friends changed. Most of the student body was unaware of what happened, but this once close group of athletes and friends who sat and visited on the stair stoops after class was now divided. Friendships fractured as people chose sides.

I cherished my friendships and struggled with the ever-present tension that now filled the school hallways. At times it felt like a war zone. No longer able to speak to old friends freely or congregate the way we once did, I was always on guard. I was protecting the friendships I still had and my sanity. I continued to excel on the track and in the classroom, but my social life was in shambles.

One morning, between homeroom and first period, Shari and I and two of our closest friends were chatting before class. One of the guys on the football team walked by and mumbled a sly comment under his breath. Shari and Raecena, the wittiest of the group, snapped back at him. I never said a word. To this day I have no idea what he even said, but the atmosphere was so tenuous that any little spark could start a fight.

He quickly grew upset, but this rage was both unexpected and frightening. Out of nowhere, he punched me in the face. We couldn't believe it, and before I could rectify what was happening and retaliate, everyone jumped in and separated us.

Everything happened in such a flurry that I had to be reminded to call Dad. I could feel his outrage through the phone. He didn't even hear the full story before he was parked on campus, but by the time he arrived, the young man was long gone.

It was probably the worst experience of my high school days, but support, particularly from my family, kept me involved in the church. I started to understand that being a Christian doesn't exempt a person from tough times and trials but invites Christ to walk along on the journey.

I focused my energy on being the best student-athlete I could be.

In the weeks leading into my senior year, I started doing an intense core routine. I'd go to the track before everyone else and run stadium stairs. I studied film. I became a true student of my sport.

My senior year was the first year I ran the 400. I set a new national record in winning the quarter mile at the National Scholastic Indoor Championships, shaving more than a second off the previous mark. My focus as I competed there was on the

200 title and record, both of which I attained, but once again my performance opened our eyes to potential and possibility, if properly nurtured.

My aunt's insistence that we move to the United States for an opportunity to attend a four-year college was beginning to pay off. Based on my performance on the track and in the class-room, college coaches visited me every weekend. It was a family dream realized.

I was pursued by Stanford, LSU, South Carolina, Miami, Florida, Tennessee, and so many others, but my favorite all along was coach Beverly Kearney from the University of Texas. Her hundred-watt smile, her swag and confidence, and her talented young team seemed like the perfect fit for me.

My high school career came full circle as I entered the final state championship meet. I began as an unknown freshman, and by my senior season, front-page pictures and big headlines felt like the norm. I never shied away from boldly stating my goals, and the media gladly covered my candor. Everyone knew I entered my senior state championships chasing new meet records in the 100, 200, and 400.

I swept the events, establishing a new record in the 400 but failing to come away with records in the 100 or 200. Silently, I was satisfied, because I knew the toll my body was undertaking by competing in so many events in leading the Raiders to a fourth team title. Still, I was just the second runner ever to sweep the 100 all four seasons, and my ten individual titles were the second most all-time in Florida history.

Mostly, I was grateful for a rewarding high school experience and the exposure it afforded me.

By the time I turned sixteen and a senior in high school, my family was fully settled and invested in Florida. I had made strong friendships, thanks to the camaraderie of track and teammates, and was earning attention for my form and race times, competing all across the country. After a summer club meet, I was approached by a woman, Joy Kimani, who thought I was talented and promising. She encouraged me to register and compete with the junior national team. I was ecstatic. In track and field, running for one's country represents the pinnacle of the sport. Think about it, when you win the Olympics, they don't play *your* favorite song on the medal stand; they play the *national anthem*. So I couldn't wait to go sign up.

"We'll need your passport, please."

I turned to my mom, and she realized immediately that we didn't have one. We were legal immigrants with a green card to live in the United States, but we weren't naturalized citizens.

If I wanted to be on Team USA, it would be a process.

Barely old enough to drive a car, I was faced with a choice I never imagined making—Jamaica or the United States? I wanted to compete for Team USA. All my friends were American, and I wanted to make the team with them. It had been four years since my family moved to live and work in Florida. Four years to a kid feels like a lifetime, and I didn't know any of the young Jamaican athletes. I begged my parents to let me join the U.S. team. They had many discussions about it. We are proud Jamaicans, but ultimately my parents thought it was the best decision for me and my future.

My mom started working toward her citizenship immediately. Once she was naturalized, Shari and I would automatically become U.S. citizens because we were minors, and I'd be eligible to compete. It's a tough process, with so much vetting and preparing. I remember quizzing Mom, a complete change of our norm, and helping her with her American history. I felt like she was doing it for me and wanted to help her as much as I could. I was elated when she passed all the tests and checks, and we became United States citizens.

Being a young and naive teenager, I could not foresee the controversy it would eventually cause.

The summer of 2002 gave me a glimpse into the future we had so purposefully fantasized. Those months between high school graduation and enrolling as a freshman at Texas allowed me to completely focus on track—no homework or group projects also requiring my attention.

Of course, as my focus intensified, so did the pressure. We traveled for the first time to Eugene, Oregon, for the prestigious Prefontaine Classic at the end of May. Known in the track world as simply "The Pre," the race is named in honor of Steve Prefontaine. He was a gutsy distance runner, and shouts of "Go, Pre" followed him around Hayward Field, the track where he competed in college for the Oregon Ducks. He died tragically in a car accident at just twenty-four, and the meet endures as a stage where runners are invited to honor him with their focus and bravery. Annually, this track reveals the breadth and depth of competitive character.

The Pre was probably the first meet of my life in which Dad didn't direct himself to a seat on top of the finish line. At one of the largest and most respected track and field meets in the United States, he didn't have to worry about making his own recording. It was on TV, aired nationally by ESPN2, and I was the only high schooler invited. He knew my race would be showcased, and Dad was more than happy to find his place some seventeen rows high in the east grandstands, in the middle of the home stretch.

Fast times and mounting buzz carried me to my first appearance at historic Hayward Field, which would quickly earn a special place in my heart. I held the fastest girls' 400-meter time in the nation, and my indoor performances that year in the 400 and 200 would have placed me among the top five against NCAA competition.

I set a new Florida state record (52.51 seconds) in winning the 400 title for my high school a few weeks prior. Chasing the national record of 50.74 was the next goal. Dad always had me looking forward, asking what's next and what's possible.

In a field that featured two Olympians and a handful of other world-class professional runners, I wasn't expected to do any better than finish last. But by identifying a tangible goal—the national junior record—I was able to stay motivated to be at my best, and that was significant at a track meet with a reputation for showcasing top prep performers like long-distance runner Alan Webb and quarter-miler Monique Henderson, who just happened to hold the record I was chasing.

The spectacle of the event opened my eyes to the enormity of my reality. When Dad and I first walked onto the track for practice, I saw Olympic stars like Gail Devers, Stacy Dragila, and Marion Jones.

"Dad, we're finally here."

I fell short of the national record, running 51.15, but surprised everyone with a second-place finish out of lane 2. The winner was eventually banned from the sport a year later for steroid use. The announcer called me back onto the track and urged me to take a victory lap. The Hayward Field crowd, some of the most knowledgeable and appreciative track fans in the world, stood and applauded.

I was stunned. They were cheering for me—after I finished second.

Only in America.

Another passionate crowd awaited me in July. What were the odds? For the first time, never before and never since, the IAAF World Junior Championships were contested at the national stadium in Kingston, Jamaica.

To get there, I won the 200 and 400 meters at the U.S. Junior Nationals, and that was no easy feat. I had to defeat Monique Henderson, the high school national record holder in the 400, and Allyson Felix, an upcoming star in the 200. I was the only one chasing the double and needed to run my best races to win.

The 400 final was contested first, and I broke Monique's national record in her hometown and maintained my status as the top-rated junior quarter-miler in the world. Edging out Allyson in a tight battle for the 200 title, I couldn't wait to head to Jamaica.

My Team USA international debut was set for a stage where I already cherished so many memories. This country—this track— helped shape me as a runner and competitor, and I anxiously hoped the appreciation I felt for the place would pour back into me. The Jamaican people, though, felt as if I had abandoned my homeland, and instead of warmth and affection, hostility greeted me as I arrived in Jamaica. It was apparent from the beginning, and at a press conference to preview the star-studded champion- ships, which also featured a young Jamaican hopeful named Usain Bolt, I could feel my nerves fraying. "I hope everybody will still love me," one newspaper quoted me as saying.

Like usual, I bore a heavy load for my team, scheduled to run the 200 and 400, as well as the 4x100 and 4x400 relays. The entire junior squad voted me team captain and elected me to be the flag bearer during the opening ceremonies. I was honored to be both but told my teammates I didn't want to offend the Jamaican fans any further. I declined the role as our flag bearer.

Still, the locals suggested I was a traitor, and boos and jeers rang out as I arrived at the stadium. I was caught off guard. Emotionally, I wasn't prepared for the negativity. Shari cried in the stands. It was ugly.

The opening heat of the 200 was scheduled just hours before the 400 final. The win-or-lose mentality that Jamaica ingrained within me reared its ugly head. I was still a young runner, and I had so much to learn about racing with strategy. In these opening heats, all you have to do is finish among the top two to advance to the next round. But I was intent on winning. A girl from Canada ran the race of her life against me. I had to set a personal best to beat her—in the first round.

What was I thinking? We were so far in front of the rest of the field, I could have geared back and walked the final meters and still moved on, but I didn't know. I was consumed with having to win, and that obsession beat me soon after.

Of course, the 400 final was a sight to behold. More than fifteen thousand fans crammed inside the National Stadium. Steel drum beats and the black, green, and gold flags of Jamaica rose into the muggy night air from the sea of people. Jamaicans love track and field and are very rarely rewarded with international caliber competition, so this event meant a lot to the people and the country. Every fan wanted to see the Jamaicans win, and unlike my Vaz Prep days, I was not wearing the right colors. The fans taunted my family.

"She nah go win!"

"She's a sellout. She don't deserve di gold."

Even though I was treated as the adversary, for the first time forced to line up as the villain, my focus didn't waver. This time, like every time I entered a race, I was set on winning. My mind and heart were ready, but my legs couldn't answer.

I ran out hard and felt strong, but when I came into the last 100 meters, there was nothing left. My energy was all gone, drained from me on this same spot a few hours earlier with that crazy kick to conquer my 200 heat. Now, when it mattered in the 400 final—when a winner was actually determined—I couldn't find another gear to match my American teammate Monique

Henderson. I looked over at her in disappointment mid-race as she passed me. How could she do this? Why would she let me suffer such embarrassment here? I was devastated.

Just past the finish line, I found Monique, hugged her in congratulations, and then slumped into a nearby chair. I was exhausted and humiliated. As I stared at the track, I berated my effort. I wanted to win; I wanted to set a personal record and prove to the people who sneered at me and taunted me that I was at least worth the effort. That I lived up to my billing. That Team USA was lucky to have me. But I didn't do any of that, and I had to be back at the track the next morning for my 200 semifinal.

I went down to Jamaica with sights set on a pair of individual gold medals but left with none. With a silver in the 400 and a bronze in the 200, I was beaten, mentally and physically. Then, to add injury to insult, I sprained my ankle during the preliminary heats of the 4x400 relay—a race I wasn't even supposed to run. I was in the stands wearing jeans and a T-shirt, supporting one of my teammates, but the team needed a quick sub in the relay. I didn't have my uniform or spikes.

In borrowed clothes and shoes, I crossed the finish line first and then promptly stepped into a covered hole and severely rolled my ankle.

It was a difficult international debut, to say the least.

Later that month, as I was preparing for the move to Austin and my start as a collegiate athlete, Mom drove me to a hotel near Miami. I put on one of my best outfits, and Mom hurried me into the car, telling me we were going to be late for a newspaper photo shoot. That seemed reasonable to me, until we arrived at the hotel, and I saw one of my uncles in the hallway.

Is this a surprise party? I wondered to myself.

It was Sanya Richards Day.

The doors to the ballroom opened, and instead of a backdrop, lights, and cameras, a roomful of people turned and applauded me. The St. Thomas athletic director, George Smith, and my high school coach, John Guarino, organized the surprise event to announce me as the 2002 Gatorade National High School Girls Athlete of the Year.

July 25, 2002, was officially named Sanya Richards Day, according to a proclamation signed by our congressman, a commendation from the city of Fort Lauderdale, and a congratulatory letter from Jeb Bush, Florida's governor at the time.

I became Florida's first track and field student-athlete to earn national athlete of the year honors, joining other Floridians like baseball stars Derek Jeter and Alex Rodriguez and football star Emmitt Smith as recipients. Joining them on that esteemed list propelled me forward. Not only was it the greatest honor of my young career, but it also motivated me to live up to expectations. The people who chose me for the award believed in my ability to move on and establish myself among the greats, and it once again validated the commitment I was devoting to my training.

It wouldn't pay off to get stuck in what was. For me, it was always necessary to flip the dial forward. A short memory pulled me out of that negative experience in Jamaica, because even though I dealt with the crowd and the losses, and for the first time struggled against defeat and devastation, I looked from the positive perspective. Eventually, I saw the Jamaicans' jeers as coming from a loving place. They were disappointed because I wasn't there competing for Jamaica, and as a competitor myself, I could understand that frustration. I embraced it and found a way to empathize. It's not a negative memory in my mind, even though it was tough to be on the receiving end.

We're all children of God, and because of that, we're all the same, regardless of where we were born, where we live, or what we look like. I learned how to be compassionate by experiencing the opposite.

PUSH

Support, God, and pressure are all needed to reach your full potential and manifest your talent.

It's important to surround yourself with people who believe in you, people who add to your journey with encouraging words, support of your dreams, and a shared positive outlook.

Those relationships are important, but nothing will compare to your relationship with God, who is always with you.

His love is what will guide you through the pressure-filled moments that create diamonds.

Chapter 3

SOLDIER STATUS

Finding Your Voice

"For I know the plans I have for you," declares the LORD, "plans to prosper you and not to harm you, plans to give you hope and a future."

JEREMIAH 29:11

The pride and winning tradition of The University of Texas will not be entrusted to the weak or the timid."

The first time I walked into the University of Texas weight room as a seventeen-year-old freshman and saw those words etched on the back wall, I knew I was in the right place. It reminded me of the feeling I had when I made my official recruiting visit as a high school runner and determined that Austin would be my future home.

Unlike my official visit to UCLA, where Monique Henderson kept calling me "the recruit," the Lady Longhorns were welcoming and friendly. Raasin McIntosh and Nichole Denby were my hosts. Raasin was a hyper, fun, crazy girl from Houston, and Nichole was a cool, calm, and collected girl from California. I just knew I wanted to be their teammate. Right away, we formed an unbreakable bond, which helped us push each other during practice and in competition.

I was young and eager when I arrived on the Forty Acres of the University of Texas campus, ready to race and train with all my new teammates as the powerhouse that was the Lady Longhorns' track and field team. National championships were the goal.

Our coach, Bev Kearney, was larger than life.

She was one of only two female black Division I head coaches in collegiate track and field, and I admired that. Until college, most of my coaches were male, aside from Mrs. June Simpson, one of my very first coaches in Jamaica, and I wanted to be around someone I could relate to and aspire to be like.

A flashy dresser and slick talker, Bev's aura was so mesmerizing that she could convince you of anything. Her style mimicked Baptist preachers and Southern grandmothers. Her sermons could come anytime, anywhere. She wanted to keep us motivated and sent us inspirational text messages and emails throughout the day. She cared about our success on the track, but like our mother away from home, she was also endearing, always welcoming us into her home. Most of the team, me included, was completely enthralled by her. She drove the nicest cars, her hair and nails manicured to perfection and her outfits coordinated down to her socks.

With Bev, it was her way or the highway.

The Texas track and field teams were not combined. The women's team was its own program. We had our own coaches separate from the men. We didn't even go to the same competitions if we didn't have to. Bev rarely spoke to Bubba Thornton, the men's head coach, and we didn't mingle or associate with the men's team.

Bev was livid when I started dating one of the guys on the track team my freshman year. She never told me I couldn't date whoever I wanted to, but I always felt like I was betraying her by entertaining someone on the guys' team. Despite her strict and rigid ways, the team bought in and wanted to please her.

She had a favorite saying. "If they aren't in burnt orange and they can't score us any points, we don't speak or interact with them," Bev preached. "When we enter a competition, we're on a mission, and it starts the moment we walk into the arena."

Her message rang out loud and clear: if you wanted to be the best, you can't be friends with everyone.

"Do you want to be respected or liked?" she'd ask us routinely and rhetorically.

Bold in burnt orange, with Texas across our chests, we formed a formidable group, whether we were coming or going. Always well dressed, because that was important to Bev and to most of us, we held our heads high and eyes forward. No one messed with us. We were the mean girls of college track and field, and we owned it. We wanted to get in people's heads before we ever lined up, and it was a tactic that didn't go unnoticed.

It was all about perception. Often mistaken as our bodyguard, Bruce Johnson, our strength coach, led the team into every competition venue. At six foot three and three hundred pounds, his presence was intimidating and imposing. Truly a gentle giant, he was a huge part of our team success.

One of my favorite experiences as a Lady Longhorn came during my freshman year in 2003 at the NCAA Indoor National Championships in Fayetteville, Arkansas.

There were two heats of the 400-meter final, and the fastest time decided the overall winner. The heats are seeded by time. I was in the fastest heat. Rarely does the time from the slower heat ever win the championship title, so I was a bit overconfident and ran my race to win as opposed to running for my best time. I won my section but lost to South Carolina's Lashinda Demus from the slower heat. I was disappointed. Winning as a freshman would have been a colossal achievement, but it motivated me for the final event of the competition, the 4x400m relay.

The Texas women always had great success on the 4x400m relay. South Carolina presented our biggest challenge, and each leg of the relay was evenly matched. The entire squad needed to run a strong race in order to win.

Despite being the youngest on the team, I called a group huddle. I channeled my inner Bev and reached within for a motivating moment. I pleaded with my teammates to dig deep and pull out a big win. We all had worked so hard and believed so fervently in Bev's plans. To embolden them, I told them our reputation was on the line. To close, I quoted my favorite slogan from the weight room wall and told my team this one was for Texas.

Keisha Downer was our first leg. She gave it everything she had and put Raasin in great position. After Raasin's leg, the race opened up, and it became a two-team battle. Moushaumi Robinson, a senior, was our third leg and raced against a career-long foe, South Carolina's Demetria Washington. They handed off the baton together, setting up a rematch between Lashinda and me. The stadium erupted. The air was electric. As I rounded the final bend, still a step ahead of Lashinda, I remember hearing Coach Bev yelling, "You got it, Sanya! Bring it home!" I turned it into overdrive and opened up a lead to win the indoor relay title.

Victorious moments like that, and we had quite a few, made

everything seem worth it. From the outside we appeared to have it all together, but internally many of the girls were crumbling.

Bev used tactics that she thought motivated us but eventually felt more like manipulation. Each week after practice, she ranked us with one to five stars.

Five stars, you're a soldier.

One star, you're a punk.

Every week, girls walked up to the locker room door, hoping to be on top of the heap, and they were shattered when they weren't.

As a consistent five-star soldier, I never noticed the damage this kind of grouping caused. It divided our team. Bev encouraged us, the soldiers, to do whatever we could to inspire our teammates to work harder and perform better.

We became menacing bullies to our teammates who weren't meeting Bev's standards.

I knew I was completely under her spell and had sunk to a new low when I walked up to one of my teammates in the cafeteria and told her she was eating us out of a national championship. It was one of Bev's favorite lines, and the moment it slipped from my lips, I knew it was wrong.

But at seventeen years old, I was so immature and malleable that I didn't stop. Like Bev, I wanted to be a champion, and her no-nonsense attitude seemed like the right way.

Raasin and I were Bev's favorites, and everyone knew it. We hung out in her office all day long. In December 2002, Bev was involved in a terrible car accident during Christmas break. She was thrown from an SUV and suffered severe spinal injuries that left her partially paralyzed. Bev coached the 2003 season from a hospital room, and Raasin and I were at her bedside almost every day after class.

Nichole also had a good relationship with Bev, but it was different. Bev was good at getting in your head and making you believe you weren't as good as you thought you were, that you needed her guidance to reach your full potential. She had the answers, the workouts, and the experience. It was her way or no way, and no one bought into that more than Nichole.

Raasin and I, though, were her pawns. Always on a mission to get everyone in formation or else.

By my sophomore year, I started to see the error of my ways. The girl who everyone bullied about eating too much had gained so much weight that she was about to lose her scholarship.

I realized we might have been going about things the wrong way. Maybe we had made her so insecure, like so many others on the team, that we were driving her to overeat. I realized that I was as much a part of the problem as Bev was.

I started to pull back. I started to stand up to Bev, and our dynamics changed drastically.

In 2004, we were scheduled to host the National Championship meet at the Mike A. Myers Stadium in Austin. We had one of the best teams in the country, and with home field advantage, we could already envision holding up the championship trophy.

I had the fastest time in the nation in the 400; Raasin was favored to win the 400 hurdles; and Nichole was a top contender for the 100 hurdles. With the three of us leading the charge, we knew if we did our part, victory was ours.

Well, everything that could go wrong did. We had the best time in the 4x100m relay, qualified easily for the finals, and were disqualified on the weirdest of technicalities. It was raining, and everyone else was using white tape as their markers on the track, but Bev gave us half-cut yellow tennis balls to use as our markers. We all thought it was legal but found out later it gave us an unfair advantage because our markings were less likely to move under the conditions.

We were counting on those ten points, and like dominoes, we all just started crashing down.

Raasin hit a hurdle in her race and finished fourth. I was third in the 400, and our team fell down—literally hit the track during the race—after we walked out in our never-before-seen, all-white full Nike bodysuits for the 4x400m relay. It was a nightmare, but there was one shining light. Nichole, my best friend, won the 100 hurdles title and broke the national record.

As a standout in high school, she ran well in college but never won a national title. It was her senior year and her last chance. It was the best race of the night for the Lady Longhorns, and although I was super disappointed in my performance, I was so happy for Nichole. She had worked so hard and deserved to be a national champion. It was her moment.

At the end of the meet after our team finished a disappointing third, Bev called Raasin, Nichole, and me over for a meeting. I just knew she was going to lay into Raasin and me, since we didn't do what was expected of us. But Bev flipped the script. She manipulated the situation and did the unexpected. She found a way to take her anger out on Nichole. I'll never forget her words. "And look at you, Nichole, walking around here like you did something. You ain't do nothing. Who'd you beat? Lo-Lo Jones?" I was crushed. I couldn't hold my tongue, which everyone did in Bev's meetings, and I spoke up.

"How could you say that? Nichole is the only one who did her part! That's not cool, Bev. That's not cool at all." I got up and walked out of the room in disbelief that the leader of our team could be so cruel to the one person who deserved her praise.

After the 2004 Olympics in Athens, I had the unique opportunity to forgo my collegiate eligibility at Texas and compete as a professional athlete with Nike as my sponsor. I was still planning to work with Bev as my coach. She insisted she would be able to train Raasin and me, along with her college team. During my first visit to the Nike campus in Portland, Oregon, as I was enjoying the best part of the trip—shopping in the employee store—I was actually looking for a gift for Bev when Mom called and told me that Bev had written her an email saying she did not want to continue being my coach. Bev wrote that she wanted to focus all her efforts on the Lady Longhorns.

I was confused and hurt and had so many questions. I called Bev, against my mother's will, and she answered my call as though she had no idea who was ringing her cell. "This is Beverly Kearney," she said. This was a woman I had called daily for two years. Someone I confided in, trusted, and loved dearly. Had she already deleted my number? She sounded so cold and matter-of-fact. I could tell our relationship was over, whether or not I was ready for it.

I was disappointed, but always knew my success in sport was not contingent on one person working with me or believing in me. I felt my success was already ordained, and all I had to do was keep working hard and believing in myself. I still had my core people supporting me. My family was always there, and Bruce Johnson was intent on working with me until the end of my career. All I needed now was a new coach.

In Athens, I watched Jeremy Wariner win the 400-meter Olympic title while only just completing his freshman year at Baylor University. As a student of the sport, Dad knew Jeremy was coached by Clyde Hart, who had guided Michael Johnson to gold medals in 1996 and 2000, as well as to the world record.

Coach Hart was universally respected as a master tactician and teacher of the 400. Of course, if I had to make a coaching change, I wanted him mentoring my budding career. There was just one problem: he had never coached an elite female to world-class or international success.

After a phone call introduction, Dad and I drove the ninety minutes north on Interstate 35 to meet Coach Hart in Waco, where he was the longtime track and field coach at Baylor. I think something in me sparked Coach's curiosity. He wanted to see if his proven philosophy would also apply in a female, and my reputation as a hard worker gave him confidence I would thrive in his training environment. We agreed to work together for one year and then evaluate the relationship. Coach Hart likes to joke that after all thirteen years of my professional career, he's still being evaluated on a trial basis. In reality, Coach Hart is one of my greatest teachers and the best mentor I could ask for in the sport of track and field.

When I started my professional career under Coach Hart, training alongside his Baylor team, my eyes were opened to a new way of doing things. The men's and women's teams were combined; they encouraged each other and prayed every day before practice. They talked to other teams and really enjoyed the camaraderie of sports.

I loved everything about my new environment except for one thing: after many of their team meetings they'd yell, "Beat the stinkin' Longhorns!"

I laughed. In my heart I always knew they might not beat the Longhorns in many events on the track, but in so many ways they were winning off the track. They showed genuine love for and support of one another. It was admirable, and I found it refreshing to be among peers who practiced in a structured but lighthearted environment marked by respect for all athletes.

Although Bev and I never worked together again, I still consider my time at the University of Texas to be some of the best years of my life. I only spent two years in the track and field program before becoming a professional, but Bruce Johnson ended up being my strength coach and mentor and one of my very best friends. I met my future husband there, and Nichole, Raasin, and I are lifelong friends.

The pressure to succeed can be intense, and I thank God for the amazing support I received from my parents, who were plugged into my progress throughout my college career. They bolstered me and allowed me to persevere in an atmosphere where many athletes are wounded.

 **PUSH**

There will always be challenges in life to push through, and sometimes they'll come in the form of people. People you love and trust may betray, but look within and remember that everything you need is already inside you.

Speak up if you feel situations are not right. This may leave you as an outsider or in the quiet minority, but trust that God is directing your path.

We must always remember that God's plans for our lives are too great to be diverted by anyone. In the end, it's only His approval we need, and only His approval we should seek.

Chapter 4

COMPETITION OF ONE

Getting Out of Your Own Way

*If anyone thinks they are something when
they are not, they deceive themselves. Each
one should test their own actions. Then they
can take pride in themselves alone, without
comparing themselves to someone else.*

GALATIANS 6:3–4

I really thought they would cancel the race. I didn't realize they sold tickets and that there was a strict schedule to maintain. I was young. It was my second world championships—my first as one of the favorites.

Looking out the bus windows, I could barely squint through the Helsinki downpour to gauge the walk awaiting the competitors up to the athlete check-in. Mind games began to overtake me. *This has to be the longest walk in track and field history*, I muttered to myself. I wanted to ask the organizers if this was some joke or botched logistics lesson. They handed us umbrellas as we stepped off the bus and started our uphill trek through a gauntlet of wind, rain, and thunder. The umbrella was sucked up into the wind, and my hoodie and rain pants were no match for the conditions. I was soaked from hair to toenails, and I hadn't even signed in to compete yet.

This can't be happening, I thought. *Surely the organizers will reschedule.* Sheets of rain covered my "oval office" in currents of water. This obsession with the uphill walk and my suddenly soaked socks really just distracted me from my main focus—Tonique Williams-Darling, the powerful runner from the Bahamas who had won Olympic gold in the 400 meters the previous summer in Athens.

In 2004, I turned professional after winning gold on the 4x400 relay at the Olympics. I didn't medal individually, but if I had run my fastest time from that season, I would have earned bronze. That validated to me that I was ready to move beyond the grinding team schedule of college athletics and pursue my potential to be one of the world's best.

Tonique was my main competition for the 2005 World Championships title contested on this water-soaked track in Finland. She beat me at a major track meet in the United States in June, but I had come back to beat her a month later during the European racing season. Tonique didn't have the physique of a typical quarter-miler. Unlike the long, lean legs I'd typically see on my competitors, she had the squatty trunk of a running back. Her whole body popped with the chiseled cut of muscle, but she always styled her hair and did her makeup like a beauty queen. When my family scouted competitors and talked race strategy, she was simply known as "Miss Maybelline."

She announced her presence at the track with a regal aura. When she and her entourage arrived that day, the rain, falling harder and heavier by the minute, seemed to slide right around her. Tonique was dry as a bone. At least it seemed that way to me.

The night before the race, I had a conversation with a runner I really admired. "To win against Tonique," he said, "you have to beat her off the curve." My youth crippled me once again, because I didn't have the nerve to say that when I won in Lausanne— the Swiss city that sits beside Lake Geneva and is home to the International Olympic Committee—I had to make up ground coming through the turn into the homestretch, the final 100 meters. But he said it, and I believed his advice. I wanted to know I'd be doing something different—something extra—to guarantee a win. I failed to see that the winning formula was inside me all along.

The rain was torrential, and it remained my tormentor. Coach Hart said it was the first and only time he'd ever seen a track covered in curling waves of water. Still, they lined us up to run. The last thing Coach told me before I walked out to my lane was, "Push, pace"—a reminder of the strategy we'd use to run every race. He always tells me to get out hard and then find my rhythm for the last half of the race. If I pace myself through the final turn, I can kick it down the homestretch, but that wasn't the advice I was given the night before.

Push, pace, whatever, I said to myself. *I'm beating her off the curve, and I'm winning this final.*

I drew lane 3, and Tonique had lane 6. Running on the inside of your biggest rival can be, and should be, a big advantage. Pacing, movement, and position all become an auxiliary sense. When it comes time to make the turn and really race, that awareness is your friend. This time, though, Tonique became my target. I fixated on her instead of my lane and my strategy. Lost in Tonique, I neglected the 4 P's.

Coach Hart's "push, pace" strategy tells me to power through the first 50 meters with everything I have and then transition after the first turn, throttle back, and preserve my best running for the end of the race. This time, though, I was intent on beating

Tonique around the last curve, and I did. But when I got there, in front of the pack, my legs were all out of running. All of my energy had been used up chasing her. I couldn't hold the lead.

It was all I could do to hang on and finish second in the world championships. For a twenty-year-old, second-year professional, that should feel like an accomplishment, but I was heartbroken. And not because I lost, but because I beat myself running someone else's race. Before I ever stepped on to the track and squinted through the downpour, eagle-eyeing Tonique, I talked myself out of winning.

It was a lesson learned. "They can't beat me if I run my best race" became a mantra I'd say before every race throughout my career. The disappointment and devastation that come when you allow the circumstances around you to create a negative mind-set were very real to me. As a young, still-maturing professional athlete, that loss in the 2005 world championships was one of the hardest things I've had to overcome. The moment I crossed the finish line, I knew I second-guessed myself to a second-place finish.

Trusting myself—who I am and what I can do—wasn't just a struggle I encountered on the track. It came into play even when I fell for the love of my life, my husband, Aaron Ross.

We started dating when we were both athletes at the University of Texas. On the track is where I feel the most pure and most at peace. It's where I learned to compete, stretch my limits, and explore my potential. On the track is also where my husband first admired me.

Ross loves to tell the story. He was in the bleachers at the Texas Relays, a huge track meet hosted at the University of Texas, and he spotted me getting ready for my race. We were both Texas athletes, but hadn't yet met. Ross pointed me out to his mother and said, "Just give me a few weeks. She'll be my girl."

A year later, though, I made the first move. I saw him in a campus cafeteria and called him over. I guess you could say the rest is history. When he took me to dinner on Saturday night and to church on Sunday, I knew he was the one.

Boys from Texas have a special swagger. They call it *walkin'*. And Aaron Ross is a true Texas boy. He's calm and soft-spoken but with enough confidence to fill a football uniform. It's attractive and also comforting how he shows so much love for his mama while appreciating the closeness of family. For me, that's everything, because family is my everything. My dad has been a lifelong mentor; my mom is my manager; and my sister is my best friend and a business partner. Today we have our own lives and families, but our three houses are within walking distance of each other. That might intimidate some guys. It made Ross love me even more.

When we met in 2003, Ross was a defensive back for the Longhorns, with his eyes set on the NFL, and our lives easily meshed together. I never had to worry about Ross tempting me with French fries, and every night when it was time for my sacred core routine, Ross happily joined in and counted for me. He understood and appreciated the discipline required when someone is training to be the best.

Our careers took off like our courtship. I turned professional in 2004, traveling to compete around the world, and Ross remained at UT. The Longhorns won the national championship the next year, and in 2006, he was named the nation's best collegiate defensive back.

When the New York Giants football team selected Ross—only strangers call Ross by his first name—in the 2007 NFL Draft, my professional career was already in full bloom. We were already dreaming together about our engagement and marriage, but some friends and family whispered to me that Ross would lose interest because I was caught up in my own career, with my own goals and championship dreams. Girls would line up, people said, just for the satisfaction of sitting in the wives' suite on NFL Sundays.

Those outside whispers became my own thoughts of insecurity. I understood how people viewed a typical NFL wife—someone who'd be there at his beck and call, satisfied to be beautiful arm candy and spend his hard-earned millions on diamonds and furs. And that wasn't me.

Ross was a catch. I had to remind myself I was a catch too.

As I raced overseas, Shari stayed at my Austin apartment, and Ross was a frequent guest. She'd often cook him dinner and watch as he'd fall asleep listening to slow jams.

"Please come home," Shari would joke with me over the phone, "so this boy can get his life back and get out of this depression."

In my heart I knew Ross was devoted to me. But the mind plays nasty tricks. My tormentor returned as another flood overcame me. Emotions and insecurity overtook me. I'd imagine all the temptations lurking around him back in the United States, and I couldn't shake the images others were planting in my head.

During our college days, a teammate gossiped to me one day at practice that she saw another girl driving Ross's car. I overreacted, crying and screaming hysterically before I even considered that I had been with Ross on the evening she was alluding to. And his car had been parked outside my apartment the whole time. But jealousy does that. If I got that upset while we were living in the same city, how could I manage when we were a world away from each other?

Once again, I had to learn to trust—trust our connection and the commitment Ross and I shared.

I was humbled after losing the world title to Tonique. Mostly, I was angry for not believing what I knew in my heart to be true: I was the fastest 400 runner in the world. A few days after the world championships race, I visited with Coach Hart and vowed to never make the same mistake again.

"Coach, I'm going to win out," I told him. "I'm going to win the rest of my races, and I'm going to be ranked No. 1 in the world." Usually the world champion always got the *Track & Field News* top ranking, but I knew if I won my final races—if I ran to my potential—I could take the top spot.

Not even two weeks later, I ran the fastest race of my life up to that point in Zurich and then closed out the season with another victory in Monaco. I ended the season ranked No. 1, and my 48.9 seconds in Zurich was the fastest time in the world that year. It also made me the youngest woman in history to ever run below 49 seconds.

Yes, Tonique raced against me both times. But it didn't matter. I ran my race.

In February 2010, when I walked down the aisle toward Ross, it felt just like I was heading toward another finish line. I was floating down the homestretch, and before me was the greatest prize I could imagine—my soul mate, my best friend, and now, finally, my husband.

Distractions threatened to break our bond, but we stayed true. Family members would say, "Ross is making enough money for the both of you. Do you have to travel so much?" "Be careful, baby; we don't want you to lose a good man."

I know as a woman it can be hard to make choices that others criticize. I struggled at times knowing if I was maintaining the right balance. I wanted to be there for Ross. I loved him more than anything. But I was a happier person and a better partner to him when I was fulfilled from pursuing my purpose. I stayed true to my sport and worked toward my dreams with everything I had.

Ultimately, you have to trust your instincts, your heart, even when the good-natured advice from others makes you wonder if there's a better way.

The woman Ross pointed to from the bleachers that day with his mother was me in my natural state. I was in my element. Vulnerable to compete, yet confident, self-assured, and ready to race. That's the girl Ross fell in love with and the one he ultimately married. I know I can't be the wife he wants me to be—the wife he deserves me to be—if I try to be someone I'm not.

Ross made me know I was the one, his only love, and reinforced to me that he was the one for me. We prayed together before every one of my races. When I'm really honest with myself, when I quiet the noise and clean out the clutter of the world, I never had to worry about another person in our relationship. There was always someone else, but it was God. Faith gave us the foundation to move forward together as husband and wife.

Our relationship started in a flurry. We moved out of the blocks fast and fell in love quickly, and even though our love was strong, it took time to find our stride together as a couple. That was mostly on me, as I listened to others and worried about opinions and gossip, when all I really needed to do was focus on Ross and how we would grow together.

On our wedding day, Ross stood resplendent in a white tuxedo, calm and strong as always, waiting for me at the altar. I walked toward him, secure in my father's clutch, poised for the move ahead. I'd be lying if I said I remember every moment, every smile, and every thought during the ceremony. It's mostly a blur. What I have, what I hold on to, is a feeling.

It felt right. It felt on time. It felt on purpose.

The path to marriage wasn't perfect, filled as it was with

unnecessary tears and doubts. But in the end, I knew we got it right, because on that day, before God, our families, and closest friends, Ross and I said, "I do."

We ran our race.

PUSH

People can be great obstacles to our success, but sometimes our greatest distractions are in our minds. Negative thoughts and false emotions lurk to knock us unsteadily out of the blocks. Self-doubt, a lack of self-worth, and an overall feeling of unworthiness exist only if we give them space within. So get out of your own way.

PACE

Create Your Rhythm

Chapter 5

TUNNEL VISION

Eyeing the Finish

I lift up my eyes to the mountains—
where does my help come from?
My help comes from the LORD,
the Maker of heaven and earth.

PSALM 121:1–2

At the start of every new season, I would sit down with Coach Hart and go over my goals for the year. At the end of every meeting, he would tell me—like a mantra—"If we can only get 1 percent better this season, you will remain the best in the world." Three hundred twenty-three days of training to shave a couple hundredths of a second off my time. For most people that would be maddening. But standing on top of that podium, realizing a lifelong dream, keeps a person motivated and inspired.

When you think about it, we're all consumed with time. Being on time, wishing we had more time, and saving time. Time is the measuring rod of greatness, and I was determined to master it.

Those little numbers on a clock are big influencers—the difference between good and great, first and last, fast and slow. And it's amazing how much the little things can keep you locked down.

In order to run your best race, you have to stay present and relaxed. You'd think the clock would be a motivator, that it would nudge you to run even faster, but it's actually a significant distraction. The clock is a constant reminder of the past. Every time the second hand ticks forward, it memorializes the past, that moment forever gone. There was a physical manifestation in my body too. Looking at the clock always forced me to tense up. It was beginning to haunt me.

As my professional career took shape, I felt like it was time to break records, and the American record was the first on my list. In 2006, I had no pressure. There wasn't a bull's-eye on my back. Even though I finished 2005 in a flurry and was ranked No. 1 in the world, I was still an unknown commodity on the circuit. Everyone was chasing Tonique, the reigning Olympic and world champion.

Mom was my main traveling companion during the European season, because she also served as my manager. Coach Hart would drop in for big races, when his responsibilities as a college coach allowed him to get away, so it was usually just me and my mom at the track and hitting the streets between races. We were on the phone basically 24/7 with Dad, who was back home. My personal goal to break the American record became a family obsession. Everyone had an opinion on strategy, and mine was to keep watching the clock.

Dad is wise, and he knows me in ways that only a dad can. He always encouraged me to win big and win young, knowing that the window to compete is sometimes unexpectedly short. His advice for avoiding regret at the end of your career entailed breaking records and winning races as early and as often as possible.

Standing between me and the record was its present holder, Valerie Brisco-Hooks, who ran 48.83 in 1984. By August 2005, I was within 1 percent of my goal after running 48.92 in the 400 meters in Zurich. Coach Hart was right: if I could improve just 1 percent, I could be the best American quarter-miler ever.

The 2006 season became all about chasing the American record. We structured our training so I'd run two or three early meets, just to get races in my legs, and then by late May or June, my times would significantly drop as I pulled back the volume and intensity of my training sessions and really focused on racing.

Sure enough, I ran 50-something in Waco to open the outdoor season, ran 49.89 in early May, and then busted out a 49.27 on June 24 in Indianapolis. Coach Hart's plan had me on target, and I was ready to attack the goal as we went overseas for the Golden League competition.

I was light and free in every race. No one expected anything of me yet. I was running these fast times, and people kept watching, disbelieving that I would be able to follow up one emphatic victory with another. But I did.

Schedules at international meets were always different. Sometimes women's events were run first, and other times the men would lead off. Jeremy Wariner, who Coach Hart also mentored in the 400, was a frequent travel and racing companion. Jeremy and I discussed our race strategy and made friendly bets about who would have the better performance. Coach Hart measured our workouts and competitions five seconds apart. If Jeremy ran 44.3 to win his race, I need to run 49.2 or better to win our bet. I always preferred to run second, so I'd know exactly what time to beat. We were both tearing it up, and many times I'd be in a race and be more concerned about beating his times than about beating my competition. It made it fun and took a lot of pressure off racing. We were both on an undefeated streak and didn't even notice it.

My fastest races felt like my easiest races. I would be able to go out hard, maintain my momentum, and distribute my speed evenly around the track. During these races, the 400 felt like a pure sprint. Minimal deceleration and the sensation that I was running my fastest at the end.

As I got closer to dropping below 49 seconds and breaking the record, I'd always look at the clock during the last few meters. I'd call Dad after each race, and he'd say, "Sanya, if you don't look at the clock, you'll run the time. The clock is slowing you down."

Dad watched my races on fuzzy, live Internet feeds on his computer, but he was able to track my eyes and see how they moved away from the finish line and to the clock in the last few meters.

What happened when I looked at the clock? My muscles tightened, tensed up, and slowed down. The body goes where the eyes go, right? So, as opposed to everything going forward, I would be shifted slightly off course because my eyes moved from the finish line, and then everything else goes a little bit slower. And because runners anticipate the line early, probably happy that the race is almost over, sometimes I'd dip my shoulder and lean before the line. But without full extension, you also lose momentum. Those subtle movements may not be easily discernible. But add them up, and it's half a second—and that's what was between me and the record.

By now, I was understanding the groove of overseas competition. My life basically consisted of racing and recovering. Every action was intended to point me to the start line in peak performance shape. Through repetition and practice, I was learning the routine and buildup that moved my mind into race mode. I valued these summer months and races, because it was then that I truly honed my craft and embraced the totality of focus required of championship performance.

My race days were strictly ordered.

An early wake-up call.

Breakfast with my family and close travel crew.

Alone time in my hotel room, a nap to reset, a shower to awaken all my senses, hair done, makeup applied, uniform on.

Race days unfolded with predictable choreography. I arrived at the track with a calculated sense of security, evident in my precise preparation.

The race inside the Olympic Stadium in Athens was the last of my season. My fitness was supreme. I held the fastest time in the world, 49.05, but I actually drew lane 7, making me the hunted instead of the hunter. My biggest competitors could set their pace off mine leaving me to run blind. It's a funny system at the World Cup, because lane assignments had nothing to do with times or rankings, but rather with country affiliation. For some reason, Team USA drew lane 7.

I considered that a disadvantage, but over the phone, my ever-optimistic father encouraged me to find a different perspective.

"Let it work for you, baby girl, because you'll have no distractions," Dad told me.

On a nine-lane track, I had just two competitors in front of me, so Dad urged me, "Pick them up early, and don't look back."

"OK," I said, and then I promised him I wouldn't look at the clock. I didn't really believe it was slowing me down that much. I enjoyed looking at the clock. I was running so well that in most of my races I was far ahead of my competition, and the clock was my only adversary. I enjoyed staring it down, demanding that it stop before 49 seconds.

Dad begged me to try something different. "What do you have to lose? We've done it your way all season. Let's try mine."

Before I settled into the blocks I told myself one last time, *No clock, all finish line, all faith.*

I'll forever remember that race. It was the most amazing feeling. I felt no fatigue, and I was sprinting the entire time. Within 10 seconds, I had passed the runners to my right, and the rest of the race was between me and my mind. Was I strong enough to eliminate distractions and stay focused?

In lane 7, I was not used to the dimensions of the track. I rarely ran in that lane. From lane 4, I know exactly my sight lines at 100 meters, 200—all the way around. But in lane 7, I was never sure exactly where I was until I came into the final 100. I was just running free, running from feel, instinct, and power.

As I sprinted down the homestretch, I maintained my promise. I was relaxed and ran through the line. Then, finally, I looked. The clock read 48.70. A new American record.

My eyes darted around the stadium and spectator stands. I was so accustomed to having my immediate family, extended family, and friends at my biggest meets when I accomplish great things. My mom was the only one who made it to Athens, and I had no idea where she was sitting. The World Cup was a smaller championship meet, not as well attended as most.

I remember looking into the stands, no friendly eyes to connect with, and thinking, *Do you all know what I just accomplished? I'm the fastest American to ever run the 400 meters.*

The race that chose me gave me the greatest gift—my name etched in the record books alongside the greats like Flo-Jo, Michael Johnson, and Jackie Joyner Kersee.

One thing the 2006 season taught me was that in order to achieve a significant goal, a clear vision and purpose were necessary. Because I was locked in on breaking the record, I was able to identify—with help and advice from Coach Hart and my dad, of course—steps along the way where I could improve, make progress, and eventually accomplish the feat.

I turned that lesson into a tool for the remainder of my career. Before each new year, I sat at my dining room table and constructed an audacious vision board. At the center of each is the cross, my constant reminder that all things are made possible through Christ and that my greatest desire is to please Him. I used my creativity to build tangible reminders of my goals. I would cut out pictures from magazines, turn gold foil into gold medals, and write motivational phrases around the border. Nothing was too crazy or off-limits. It was an expression of my happiness and eagerness to do the hard work.

The vision board is something that allowed me to narrow my focus. It also challenged me to get clear on what I wanted. What I like best about the process, if done the right way, is that it forces you to dig deep within yourself.

What has God put me on this earth to accomplish? Who am

I supposed to touch, be an example for, or serve and support with my talents and gifts? My vision board was always on display, and I was able to mentally prepare for or reflect on each day. What is my plan today? Did my actions align with my goals? Am I progressing?

For me, the vision board is very powerful. Not only because of the time and tedious work required to create it, but also because it was a gentle motivator, a way I could push myself to make sure I was giving my very best each new day. That's the simplest way I found to tackle these crazy goals and lifelong dreams. Some days will feel better, stronger, and easier than others, but as long as we give what we've got, we'll stay on pace.

I felt that way on the track too. The narrower the focus, the better. You'd never imagine that the clock, the ultimate decider in my races, could distract me, but it did. Focus was as important at the start as the finish. For those crucial first 50 meters of the race, I'm looking as close as I can to my body. My eyes carry maybe 10 yards ahead of me. If I look around and see my competition, it just causes anxiety, and the lane feels claustrophobic.

Stay committed and true to your path, because distractions will come at you in all forms. Each day we have decisions to make. Every day is the outcome of thousands of decisions. This or that? Right or wrong? Left or right? Heels or sneakers? Each and every day, we have the opportunity to move closer to fulfilling God's plan for our lives.

When we step into the grace of God, we step out of the confinements of time. God exists outside of time and space, which is why He's not limited by them. He can accomplish in a moment what would take a lifetime, which is why His vision is too great to be limited to a piece of poster board.

It's beyond comprehension or imagination. The beauty of eternal life is that we never have to look at the clock again. Our gaze should only be pointed in a single direction: to the undefeated Champion of champions.

PACE

The narrower your focus, the better. Side projects and other goals feel like they're helping you to get to the finish line, but the truth is that it takes tremendous focus, patience, and discipline to achieve your dreams.

Stay true to your path, because distractions will come at you in all forms, in objects and places you least expect.

My sister and me

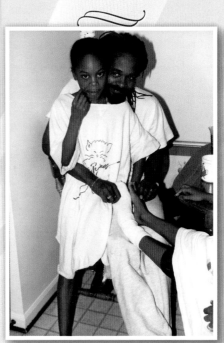

My dad and me as he massages my mom's and sister's feet

Winning the 60-meter race against Vanessa while at Vaz Prep

My freshman year at St. Thomas Aquinas

My baptism at age thirteen at ChristWay Baptist Church

Named 2002 Gatorade High School Athlete of the Year

Pep talk from Dad before
competing at the Junior
Nationals in Raleigh,
North Carolina

Dad's Prefontaine Classic ticket

Competing at the
Texas Relays

Training session with
Coach Clyde Hart

Supporting Ross after one of his UT football games

After breaking the American record in the 400 meters at the 2006 World Cup in Athens

In transition—the 4x400 relay handoff in Osaka, Japan, 2007

Start of the 400-meter race at the 2008 Olympics in Beijing

My disbelief that I blew it

My determination to win for my team at the 2008 Olympics

Gold medal presentation with my 4x400
relay team at the 2008 Olympics

Wedding day, February 26, 2010

Victory in London in the 2012 Olympic Games

Victory lap at the
2012 Olympics

My farewell at the 2016 Olympic
Trials in Eugene, Oregon

Chapter 6

FALLEN STAR

Staying Disciplined

"All this I will give you," [the devil] said [to Jesus],
"if you will bow down and worship me."

MATTHEW 4:9

M arion Jones was my biggest hero in the sport of track and field.

And that meant a lot for me.

I didn't admire many women outside of those in my family because it was never just about great performances for me. I wanted to admire people because of who they are. Contributors to society, great leaders, humble servants, and avid believers.

My dad is a passionate follower of sports. He's aware and knowledgeable about every form of competition, from mainstream NBA to European specialties like cycling and rugby. Dad revered individuals for their accomplishments and ability to play and perform. But he wasn't prone to hanging posters or holding up idols.

Integrity means everything. My family made sure I knew that.

As I readied to travel to my first World Indoor Championships in 2006, I was excited to be part of my third national team. I was starting to feel like a true professional.

I couldn't believe it when I saw Trevor Graham in the waiting area by the gate.

From the first time I saw him at the 2002 Prefontaine Classic as a high schooler, I wanted to meet him.

Everyone knew him. He coached Marion Jones, along with a plethora of other bright stars. He was the man. I wanted to pick his brain. I always loved learning from the experts in my field. I was never shy and was the first person to introduce myself and strike up a conversation in hopes of building a relationship that would be mutually beneficial.

I changed my seat on our charter flight to Russia and talked to him the entire way. He was intriguing, smart, and friendly.

"You want me to come work with you?"

"You think I can be better than Marion?" I asked, trying to keep my jaw from hitting the floor.

"After you're done dominating the 400 meters, let me coach you, and I'll make you equally as dominant in the 100-meter sprint. You're the perfect body type—tall and explosive. You're stronger than most short sprinters and not afraid of the work.

"You'll be bigger than Marion."

I hung on every word.

I always thought I'd run the 400 for a few years, win the Olympic gold, and then go back to the 100- and 200-meter sprints. They were my favorite races—where I got my start and dominated for most of my young career.

The thought of training with Marion Jones and Trevor Graham was compelling—very compelling.

The 400 is a tough race, and it's also difficult to become world-famous running the event. Most people know the athletes who win the 100 final, but it takes a whole lot more for people to remember the other events.

If you could win the short sprints, the endorsements and opportunities were endless.

I called Mom and told her about my visit with Trevor. Always the even-keeled, less radical one, she wasn't overly excited.

"I don't know about that group, San. Too many rumors swirling around them all the time," she said.

"But, Mom, he's Marion's coach. She's been running fast since she was a kid. She's a child prodigy too."

I can't even begin to put into words how much it hurt me on October 5, 2007, when Marion Jones appeared in front of a podium in a black suit and white blouse and admitted to the world that she had used performance-enhancing drugs.

I had defended her in so many trackside debates, saw myself and all that was possible in her success, believed in her abilities. I felt she had betrayed me.

It felt personal.

I wanted to feel compassion for her, but I was angry.

Angry that she didn't have the courage to say no to drugs. Angry that she didn't believe in herself the way I believed in her.

She was a once-in-a-lifetime athlete. In high school, she was the Gatorade Athlete of the Year because of her success on the track, and then she went to North Carolina and won a national championship with the basketball team. She was that good.

I believe that Marion could have still had a remarkable track career, competing in multiple disciplines, and even if she didn't win all her races, she would have won most of them—and that would have been OK. That would have made her a hero. It would have shown young girls like me what success actually looks like. Not a rocket shooting straight up, but a roller coaster with high and lows that are as challenging and exhilarating as you can find at any amusement park.

But this idea of being perfect, winning every race, and getting all the money became more important than standing for something.

As a competitor that's infuriating. Just consider how many athletes who did it the right way, who meticulously trained and planned their nutrition and devoted their minds and bodies to the pursuit and who were denied the opportunity to even line up because Marion was in the field.

In track and field, the winners claim all the glory. Especially when you're as big as Marion Jones. She had all the sponsors, from Nike to American Express. She commanded the highest appearance fees and was on the covers of all the magazines. No one else existed.

I wanted to still love her. I wanted her to walk away a hero.

Now it was time for her to own her truth. No more deception. No more lies.

Tell us that the pressure got to you. Tell us you feared losing and wanted to make your sponsors and country proud. Say you got greedy, arrogant, misled. Anything—just own it.

Instead she went on *Oprah* and told us once again she didn't know she was doping.

I was disappointed.

Still she taught me the importance of choices. I knew then and there that if I ever became a role model for young girls, I'd treat them the way I wanted Marion Jones to treat me.

I'd think of them individually.

I'd give them something real and tangible they could hold on to.

A picture of success that was attainable and true.

I never wanted anyone to have a reason to rip my posters off their wall or strip my medals away.

After my airplane meeting with Trevor Graham, I never had any interaction with anyone closely associated with drugs. I truly believe it's because of the people I had around me. Most people were probably deathly afraid of my dad, but they also saw that we were a family that believed in the fundamentals of hard work.

Even when not in the lane next to you, the remnants of cheaters' performances always linger. Take the women's 400 world record, for instance. I always wanted to be the world-record holder. The best female quarter-miler ever. But the record was so out of reach that it always seemed impossible.

If you look at most record books, times gradually drop. As technology gets better and techniques are refined, the performances progressively improve. But in the 1980s, the 400 women's record was demolished, with three seconds shaved off the time in a ten-year span. Compare that against the men who, in a span of twenty years from 1968 to 1988, only lowered the record by six hundredths of a second.

What Marita Koch did simply doesn't happen, and many experts attribute it to the excessive use of steroids during that time. In October 1985, the East German runner Koch ran 47.6 at the World Cup in Canberra, Australia, to set the world-record time. It's a full second faster than my American record. No one has come close to breaking it. No one has even run sub-48 since then. Marie-José Pérec, the long-limbed French runner, came the closest when she won her second 400 gold medal at the Atlanta Olympics in 48.25.

If there wasn't so much speculation regarding the world record, I'd be much more settled with my place in history. We know that Marita Koch competed in an era when East Germany was known to be systematically doping its athletes, and many of Koch's East German peers who raced with and against her have since admitted they doped in the state-sponsored program administered by the country's secret police.

Following German reunification in 1990, records were made public, detailing substances and quantities, and who received them. A book was later published that contained doping data for East German athletes, including Koch, though she never failed a drug test and has never publicly admitted to doping. The World Anti-Doping Agency isn't able to investigate these claims due to their statute of limitations clause.

The record stands, though it remains clouded in suspicion. I believe it was a record that was created in a lab.

Dad, a Rasta, believed in eating from the land. He faithfully juiced vegetables and fruits for me to supplement my diet, which he also oversaw like a hawk. My family didn't eat pork or red meat, and we'd fill our plates with colorful vegetables, fruits, and whole grains.

"We nuh cheat," Dad would say. "A natural ting dis." Then he'd hand me a tall glass of rainbow-colored juice—the bittersweet essence of spinach, beets, oranges, ginger, and the like. I'd hold my breath and gulp it down. These were my steroids, my edge, my natural performance enhancer.

Throughout my career, the recipe for success was never simple, but it was straightforward. Dad and Mom never allowed me to believe there was a magic pill or formula. Everything revolved around commitment and discipline. It wasn't easy. I've expended plenty of blood, sweat, and tears on a track. The reward of standing atop the podium, knowing that hard work does pay off, is one of life's best gifts.

How can we keep future generations from losing that hope? There's a power in believing in something unseen, an outcome that isn't promised. Each day you work in the faith that genuine effort will have a payoff.

As I matured in my track career, that's what nagged at me so much about Marion Jones's doping scandal. She was the face of our sport. She transcended that 400-meter oval through her story and victories, and she challenged the notion that girls had to compete within a box.

Win an NCAA basketball championship as a freshman. Drive for five gold medals at the Olympics. Anything is possible. Dream it, see it, do it.

But you can't do it clean. You need a shortcut. That's what Marion also taught us. Marion taught us to work for the medals, the money, and the magazine covers. And those things are temporary. They go away.

The International Association of Athletics Federation (IAAF) nullified all of Marion's results after September 2000, including her Olympic titles. The International Olympic Committee stripped her of those five medals won in Sydney. She went to jail.

PACE

Sometimes the idea of winning or being the best clouds our judgment. We desire more—more money, more power, and more things. We become fixated on a destination and mesmerized by what we believe will come with the new level of success.

The true prize is in the journey, the ups and downs, the character we develop along the way. Even the moments that hurt the most are crucial to your development. Don't be afraid of the hard work, the failures, the disappointments. They only make your destination that much sweeter.

Chapter 7

SPRINT QUEEN

Getting Back to Basics

No discipline seems pleasant at the time,
but painful. Later on, however, it produces
a harvest of righteousness and peace for
those who have been trained by it.

HEBREWS 12:11

After my dominant 2006 season, everything changed.
Requests rolled in every day. My mom, now my manager, was mostly overwhelmed just trying to keep up with emails and contractual commitments.

One of the requests, however, was too good to turn down.

During the offseason, before the 2007 training cycle began, I was offered a generous appearance fee to make a three-day trip to Japan. It all seemed too good to be true, and this request did not include competing.

They wanted me to be their guest, go to their most prominent restaurants, take part in cultural ceremonies, and run with the locals. It all seemed easy enough to me. Mom and I agreed and we set off in our first-class seats to Tokyo, Japan.

As an athlete, I had the tremendous luxury of traveling the world. I'd been to some of the most beautiful cities but rarely had an opportunity to see more than the hotel and the stadium. It was work, and I was always on a mission.

This trip sounded incredible.

I'd be a guest, not focused on beating the competition but on simply enjoying the experience.

First up, the restaurant—and just like on TV, we took off our shoes and sat on the ground in front of one of the largest feasts I'd seen outside of Thanksgiving dinner. Cameras rolling, all eyes on me—and I didn't recognize a thing. Most of the cuisine looked alive. I was horrified. Already a selective eater, not eating red meat or pork . . . or crab . . . or lobster, it was hard for me to find meals in America, much less selecting from octopus and sushi. I did my best—closing my eyes and eating what I could. They were such accommodating and friendly people, and I didn't want to offend anyone.

I was scheduled to be a part of a fun community race, or at least that was my understanding of it. Something was lost in translation, however. This was no fun run; this was a serious event. Most of the participants prepared the entire year for the event.

It was a four- or five-mile course in which four people ran different distances before being crowned the winner. The kicker is that the teams are handicapped. The slowest entrants went off first, while the fastest team was instructed to take off last. There was prize money, and the women on my team worked hard—they were aspiring professional track and field athletes, and this money meant a lot. A total of $4,000 would go to the winning team.

The pressure was on.

I hadn't started training yet, and I was scheduled to run 1,200 meters. I panicked. I don't even run that far in practice. How was I supposed to run the anchor leg on a handicapped team against men and women who looked forward to this event like it was their Olympics?

I was a part of a team. I had to step up. I'll never forget the race. My translator kept me abreast of all the trash talk and interactions.

On the big screen inside you could watch the race unfolding. By the time I was up, there was only one man to beat. I took off a little too fast, full of adrenaline and excitement. There were people lined up on the street, waiting to give high fives and cheer us on. When I rounded the final curve back to the building in front of the audience, I literally thought I was going to faint.

My tank was empty, but the gentleman behind me was too close to let up.

I gave it everything I had and won for my Japanese teammates. I decided not to take my cut of the prize money. I had such a great season the year before, and this race was really for them. I wanted them to get as much as they could. They were so grateful.

After the race, my mom couldn't hold it together. She laughed so hard that I couldn't help but join in. What had we gotten ourselves into?

The entire experience was awesome, but I realized then that my position in the sport had changed, and I wasn't sure I was ready for it.

Before the 2007 season started, I decided I wanted to be the Sprint Queen. I had dominated the 400 so easily, or at least that's what it felt like. I wanted a different challenge.

I wanted to get better in the 100 sprint and dominate the 200 and 400 sprints.

Only one American woman had ever won Olympic gold in both, and Michael Johnson, Coach Hart's world-record-setting protégé, had done it at the 1996 Atlanta Games. So I thought, *Why can't I?*

But my intentions weren't completely pure. I didn't only want to switch my focus from the 400 because I genuinely wanted to win other events; I switched my focus because the pressure of repeating my performances of the 2006 season seemed daunting and overwhelming.

Sometimes after we've stretched ourselves and achieved new levels of excellence, we fear going back there.

In 2006, I was undefeated, ran nine times under 50 seconds— more than all the women competing that season combined—set the American record, was named the world female athlete of the year, and was the cover girl on our coveted track and field news magazine.

I always wanted to be that girl, but uneasy lies the head that wears the crown.

I thought if I went out on a different mission, I couldn't fail.

Well, I was wrong. I went into the 2007 season as the poster girl, and I imploded.

Disaster. At the U.S. National Championships in Indianapolis in late June, I finished fourth in the 400 and ran one of my slowest races since college. *What? Are you kidding? I go from winning races by tens of meters to not just losing but coming in fourth?*

At the time of the season when Coach Hart's cycle kicks in and my times start to fall, I slowed down. How does that happen? I lost focus, that's how.

Mentally I wasn't there. I was shifting mind-sets between the 100, 200, and 400. Even though it's only a few hundred meters difference, the races are completely different. They require totally different engines and strategies.

In trying to spread my wings, I pulled my focus away from my calling and original passion. Becoming the best quarter-miler in the world is what solidified my commitment. When I diffused that mission by needlessly and selfishly adding to it, I faltered. My climb was intense. Straight up. A meteoric rise, and it created false expectations in my mind. I thought the line to success was a direct path. Every step I had taken led me to the next one. But 2006 set the bar so high that I wasn't sure I could reach the next rung on the ladder.

I bailed myself out by adding to my plate in case I wasn't able to meet that same standard of success. In doing so, I lost my purpose, and I lost my race.

PACE

Life can lure us into this fantasy. A fantasy of fear. We look around and begin to fear we aren't good enough for the right here and right now, so we create illusions in our minds of what we still need to be—when all we need to be is present in this moment, at this time.

Our purpose is singular. We all share in it. To be bright stewards of God's grace. It sounds like a simple task, and maybe that's what's scary. Because it's not simple at all. It's a daily journey that requires focus and commitment.

Other missions and visions clutter our outlook. God calls us, and our response is to transform through the stages of learning, doing, refining, and also teaching. By turning our attention away from our primary purpose, we also inhibit our growth.

Chapter 8

WINNER'S GLOW

Going with Life's Flow

The tongue has the power of life and death.

PROVERBS 18:21

There are a couple things that signify you've made it in your sport: huge corporate sponsors and rubbing shoulders with megastars.

Both were happening for me.

AT&T signed me as one of their ambassadors going into the 2008 Olympic Games, and NFL great Deion Sanders was scheduled to film a commercial at my parents' house.

It was the biggest production I had been a part of up to that point in my career. Emails zipped back and forth, permits secured to block the streets, park trailers, host camera crews and producers—the works. I loved being in the spotlight on and off the track, and the AT&T "Home Turf" trailer was an awesome opportunity to connect with more fans.

About a week prior to the event, I had my first bout of mouth ulcers that were so painful I couldn't talk. Out of nowhere, my mouth was full of frightening white pustules that were so uncomfortable I couldn't even drink water. I went to my doctor, and he prescribed an ointment that seemed to do the trick. I also showed him a lesion on my skin that was unfamiliar. He thought they were unrelated and gave me another ointment for my chest.

The night before Deion was scheduled to come to town, the

painful ulcers flared up again. They made it so difficult to open my mouth that I wasn't sure I'd be able to do the interview.

I broke down and cried. So much had gone into the production that I couldn't imagine letting everyone down.

For Olympic athletes, sponsorship opportunities were few and far between. Only being relevant and valuable to a corporation once every four years, we felt the pressure of wanting to deliver. Wanting to be memorable enough and pleasant enough to get the opportunity again in the future.

I *had* to do it.

My mom was so worried. Concerned more about my health than anything else, she became frantic.

"San, this isn't normal. We should go to the emergency room."

But I wanted to meet Deion Sanders, and I wanted to fulfill my commitment.

I prayed to God, asking that He clear up my ulcers, if just for a day, and I'd get back to the doctor as soon as I could.

He answered my prayers. My adrenaline and excitement fueled me to put on a brave face and a smile. Everything else about the day was perfect, but in the back of my mind, I was concerned that this issue might be more serious than I first thought.

I only had a week reprieve before the mouth ulcers came back.

Why didn't the ointment work?

What was happening?

These symptoms were the start of a really tough time in my life.

Besides the horrible mouth ulcers, massive lesions spread over my skin. They started on my legs and eventually presented on my arms, back, and stomach. It looked like my skin was poisoned.

As soon as one sore healed, another would appear.

The pain of the lesions was unbearable, but the reality of having to step on the track with what felt like a modern-day leprosy was even scarier. Our uniforms left so little to the imagination, and I was horrified.

For so long I took for granted the confidence that came from having great skin and a toned body. I was an athlete who ate well and worked hard and as a result was always fit and in shape. People always commented on how awesome my arms were, how they "envied my legs," and how they would "die for my six-pack." Little did they know, I almost did, every day. It was my normal, and I never thought twice about it.

Now for the first time I was terribly insecure.

Mom and I went to great lengths to cover the lesions and the scars they left in their wake. We tried bandages, makeup, everything you can imagine. It was really tough. When Nike delivered my racing kits for the season, Mom opened the package, and a smile appeared on her face.

"Look how God works for you," she said.

She pulled from the box a set of newly designed compression arm sleeves. I couldn't believe it. My arms were affected the most, and now I'd be able to cover them in a way that wouldn't seem awkward or forced. They became a trademark look after a while, but I was initially so grateful to wear them because they hid my secret, my flaws.

I crisscrossed the country for months looking for a doctor. We visited an infectious disease doctor in Austin, an ear, nose, and throat specialist in Maryland—almost every kind of doctor there was—looking for someone who could answer the question of what was happening to my body, what germ or virus was causing me to look and feel like this.

Finally, we saw a doctor in New York who said it looked like Behçet's disease, an incurable, rare, and chronic autoimmune disorder.

There were no specific tests to confirm the disease; usually a diagnosis is based on your symptoms, but sometimes doctors ordered a certain test to see if it would come back with a positive result. The doctor inserted a clean needle in my forearm and told me if I had a lesion or small red bumps in the area within the next two days, it was likely I had Behçet's.

Two days later, I was back in the office. It only took a day, and my skin exploded again like it had done many times before. As we got ready to leave the office, the gentleman at the front desk asked, "Do you have it?" His words seemed so cold and morbid. It felt like a death sentence.

I wasn't sure what it meant for me or my career. I was so confused. Behçet's affected individuals mainly in Asia and the Middle East. How did *I* get it?

Amidst my many questions, I was relieved to have a diagnosis and a road map for treatment, but my symptoms never fully disappeared. The medication made it manageable at times, but I would suffer with the symptoms for more than seven years.

After I set the American record in 2006, my endorsement career finally took off. Nike, my sponsor since day one of my professional career, began to feature me prominently in campaigns, and the requests for photo shoots and public appearances came in day after day. It was a dream.

In track and field, the prize money awarded for winning races is modest and only flows in during competition season, so to support your income, sponsorships are coveted. I perceived increasing responsibilities to my sponsors as rewards for all of my hard work. With Mom as my manager, I stressed the importance to her, and we rarely declined a request. My schedule grew jam-packed. I'd juggle weight room work, training on the track, and recovery sessions, along with a list of business commitments. I was always on the move.

As my skin was being ravaged on the outside, I internally boiled as well. I was scared. I felt lost. Every appearance was a marathon. Mom and I strategically picked outfits that covered my ulcerated skin, and we tediously applied makeup to camouflage any spots on my limbs that were exposed. Racing became an even greater task, because our aerodynamic uniforms are, by design, minimal at best.

I was constantly hiding and holding this secret shame. I detested that my body was betraying me, and I did everything I could to prevent it from disrupting public perception. I didn't believe I could measure up to my mind's translation of society's expectations for what a strong, athletic female should look like.

Nike asked me to come to its headquarters in Oregon for wear testing and a photo shoot for its latest product line. You'd think I'd be through the roof with this news, but I met this invitation with fear and concern. In that setting—around all those cameras, designers, and handlers—there was no way my marked-up skin would go unnoticed. My body would eventually betray me and reveal the truth.

Still, Mom and I devised a plan to do our best with cover-up foundation and powder. We arrived on the sprawling Nike campus for the shoot, and the setup was epic. They pulled out all the stops for this one. Lights and backdrops and people running this way and that. *All this for me*, I thought, and I was grateful—before my stomach tightened and the fear returned.

In the dressing room, I laid my head on Mom's shoulder. She held me as I let out a long breath.

"Mom, mi tiyad."

"Yuh alright, baby. It will be fine," she told me.

I walked out, bared it all, and stood in my truth. It was difficult yet freeing, all at the same time. Most people were kind enough to not stare; others couldn't help themselves, but I quickly told the room about my condition, smiled, and got to work.

This experience changed me. I was more compassionate and understanding of what many women felt every day. I became increasingly aware of the messages being sent to us every day, whether overtly or subliminally.

PACE

Pace is all about rhythm. It's about finding a routine that enhances your chance for success. Many times we think of our routines as the things within our control, like training five days a week, preparing for competition, or studying every night for exams. We also have to be aware of the subconscious routines in our lives.

Behçets forced me to face my own perceptions of beauty, to be uncomfortable and become more compassionate to individuals who deal with body image. It gave me an opportunity to examine many larger issues as well and check on my relationship with the community at large.

It's a daily struggle, but be careful of who you associate with, the music you listen to, and the images and messages you partake of, because they also affect your rhythm.

POSITION

Go with Courage

Chapter 9

MEETING GRACE

Knowing You're Always Loved

Who shall separate us from the love of Christ?
Shall trouble or hardship or persecution or
famine or nakedness or danger or sword?

ROMANS 8:35

W hat happened?" the enthusiastic Chinese official asked me. "We already had your name on the gold medal."

Trust me, I saw my name on the gold medal too.

This was the crest of the climb. Finally, a finish line. Since Dad first uttered the words when I was nine years old, everything I did was in pursuit of this vision. To win the Olympics, wear the gold medal, and complete the journey from child prodigy to Olympic champion.

And when you look at all the phases, victory at the 2008 Olympics in Beijing was the obvious crowning achievement.

Leading into those games, I was on a tear. Nothing could stop me. I was "all the way up" and feeling blessed. So what happened? How did I end up with a bronze, when gold was obviously in my future?

For most of my career, I've answered this question with half-truths.

I didn't get much sleep. It wasn't meant to be. I felt a cramp in my hamstring.

I've repeated these things on so many occasions that I started to believe them. I wanted to believe them.

This is the real story—one I haven't told. This is the story of how my bronze medal taught me my most valuable lesson. This is a story of God's grace.

For most of my life, I felt like an upstanding "Christian." I honored the word of God and did my best to approach every decision and confront every obstacle from a place of love. But the 2008 track season forced me to make one of the most difficult decisions of my life.

With this decision, I realized the frailty of the human condition. I experienced how vulnerable we can become in a split second, and it turned my understanding of God's grace upside down.

My hope is that it exposes you to the limitless depth of God's love.

After years of prayer and times of fasting, now finally ready to write this chapter, I hold tightly to the truth of my calling. By bearing my weakness, by exposing my struggle with sorrow and shame, by quieting the voice that belittles me into silence, I believe I can reach someone right where they are.

"On Christ, the solid rock, I stand; all other ground is sinking sand." Thanks to Sunday school and church choir practice, I've been singing these words most of my life. But it took me some time to grasp their meaning.

The 2008 Olympic Games exposed the small cracks in my spiritual foundation and forever changed my perception of who God is.

Many times we see God's commandments as strict rules to keep us away from the best things in life, but they are really just the Father's loving guidelines to keep us away from pain and sorrow.

When I met Ross in 2003, I knew that something in my heart had changed. Our first date was to Bennigan's, a local restaurant, but our second date was to church. Our priorities were the same, and I knew I had found love, the fire that would burn brightly for the rest of my life. I knew early on that Ross would be the one I'd marry. When Ross proposed to me, he said he waited until he signed his NFL contract so I wouldn't have to buy my own ring.

He was perfect. Loved the Lord, loved his family, worked hard, and loved sports. We were both just getting started in our careers, and the dreams of all we could accomplish together felt like a fairy tale.

Because of this, we knew it was equally important to plan for a family. Yes, I knew that abstinence until we were actually married was what God wanted for our relationship, but I started to take birth control a few months after we met. Through 2006, I battled some serious feminine issues as my body reacted to the NuvaRing, my chosen contraceptive. I was constantly in pain. I missed workouts to visit different gynecologists for ineffective treatment after treatment. It was tumultuous.

I thought about taking the pill, but I'd seen so many teammates struggle with the water weight and changes in their body that I feared the adverse effects it might have on my speed and endurance. I wanted to do the right thing and protect myself from unplanned pregnancy, but I was unaware of all my birth control options and ashamed to talk to my mother or coaches.

I was naive and in love.

From 2006 to 2008, Ross and I had full confidence that our

system was working well. We were no longer on birth control, but we trusted our plan had no issues and believed my high training load and low body fat also controlled my hormone levels.

So you can imagine the horror and shock when one month before the Olympic Games, an experience that is supposed to bring tremendous joy instead brought instant fear. The kind of fear that grips your mind, body, and spirit. A fear that envelops you just underneath the skin, rising as hot fire. The kind of fear that zaps your strength and pushes you to a powerless panic.

Ross had already gone back for training camp with the New York Giants. I called him repeatedly on his cell phone until he finally got out of practice. By the time he got back to me, I could barely get the words out through my tears.

"I'm pregnant."

"You're what?"

"I'm pregnant, babe, and I have to leave for Beijing in less than two weeks."

After a long pause, as I sensed him carefully measuring his words, he said, "How could this happen? We were so careful."

"Don't worry, babe; everything will be OK."

And I really wanted that to be true.

I believe we're soul mates. We had planned everything. Ross had already proposed to me, and we set our wedding date for my twenty-fifth birthday on February 26, 2010. There was no way I could plan a wedding during my run-up to the Olympics, and 2009 was out of the question as well. It was a World Championships year, and winning both titles, back-to-back, was the goal.

Now add a baby to the mix? I couldn't fathom it.

What do we do now?

Over the phone, we didn't go into details. As if not saying it would alleviate some of the guilt and the shame.

He wouldn't be there with me. He was in training camp, and nothing interrupted Tom Coughlin's schedule for the Super Bowl champions. Nothing.

We had fallen into this together, but I bore the physical consequences alone.

I knew I was at a crossroads. Everything I ever wanted seemed to be within reach. The culmination of a lifetime of work was right before me. In that moment, it seemed like no choice at all. The debate of when life begins swirled through my head, and the veil of a child out of wedlock at the prime of my career seemed unbearable. What would my sponsors, my family, my church, and my fans think of me?

Somewhere we all draw a line. Usually, we draw the line right behind the sin, after we've taken one step too far, before we fall past the point of no return. In the days, weeks, and moments leading up to the Beijing games, I rationalized my life against my situation. Where was my line?

POSITION

My whole life has been about running against the clock. The time between Olympic Games makes each one so important that seizing the chance to participate is often a once-in-a-lifetime achievement. No one is guaranteed even one Olympics, and I was finally the favorite, primed to stand on top of the podium. It had been my only consistent dream since I was a little girl, and the unknown of another four years was enough to keep me from taking the chance.

I had lined up against some of the sport's biggest and fiercest competitors. I had even run against cheaters, but this was the biggest giant of them all. It was me against my sport. Against myself.

I will always say it was one of my greatest blessings to be a professional athlete, and I treasure the lifelong lessons and relationships the sport has afforded me. But the dark reality of being a professional female athlete was becoming clear. Just as I neared the peak of my earthly climb, I had to turn back and see how far I could actually fall.

Most of the women I knew in my sport have had at least one abortion. Prioritizing athletic goals over the gift of life was the norm. It was all around me, but not until it was me did I realize many of these young women only wore a mask of indifference for something I can now testify requires deep thought and proper counsel.

During the car ride to the clinic, I felt both relief in the decision I had made and panic in what was to come. I entered the clinic composed, yet I was filled with an inner turmoil. All of the crying leading up to that moment had left me so numb that I barely remember the cold instruments as they brushed against my skin, and the emptiness that followed. It was a quick procedure, but it felt like an eternity.

I made a decision that broke me, and one from which I would not immediately heal. Abortion would now forever be a part of my life. A scarlet letter I never thought I'd wear. I was a champion—and not just an ordinary one, but a world-class, record-breaking champion. From the heights of that reality I fell into a depth of despair.

But like the champ I was conditioned to be, I boarded my flight to Beijing the very next day. My mom figured it might be too much to handle a fifteen-hour journey with all of my USA teammates, so she planned my flight with one of my best friends, Bershawn Jackson. We had been friends since I was sixteen years old, and he was the friend who could make any situation better. No matter how dire or awkward my circumstances were, he always made me smile. I didn't tell him for a few years, but he had no idea how much he helped me that day. We talked about our journey from the World Juniors in Kingston to becoming two of the most dominant one-lappers in the sport. We were heading to Beijing to finish what we started, and he helped me smile through my pain.

The doctor had recommended two weeks with no activity, but that was an order I couldn't follow. I didn't tell my coaches, my father, or anyone on Team USA. I landed in Beijing determined to bring home gold. Winning was the only medicine I thought I needed, and I was ready for that medication. I bottled up my sorrow in the deep recesses of my mind. For a brief moment, I felt free.

The first day of competition went well. I was on autopilot,

but instead of just outrunning my competition, I was hoping to outrun myself, and the now uncomfortable feeling of living in my own skin. I won my semifinal round, but my conscience could not be defeated.

The night before the final, my mind worked in overdrive. I couldn't shut it off. Shari recalls me babbling foolish nonsense during dinner. Shari had observed my career as completely as anyone, attending every grade school practice and traveling to most of my college and pro meets.

The feeling in the pit of her stomach spoke clearly.

"Something isn't right. I feel like she's falling apart," Shari said to Mom.

She continued to worry all the way back to their rented apartment where she and Mom were staying. Shari never went to sleep that night.

Neither did I.

As I lay in bed, in the early morning hours on August 19, 2008, I tossed and turned. Visions of the race kept me up all night.

I could never get comfortable. I kept fluffing my pillow, adjusting my sheets.

One o'clock. I'm wide awake.

Two o'clock. My roommate's asleep. Why can't I sleep?

In this fog, I could sense my soul was fully awake, dreaming of what should be. Usually when I dream, I enjoy the finishes of my races and running across the line. This time was different. It was bizarre. I just kept seeing the first 300 meters over and over again. It was like my heart wasn't ready for the finish.

My mind had so activated my body that I could feel a thin film of sweat covering me in an oily blanket. Conscious but exhausted, I could barely discern what was a dream and what was real. Looking around the room, I prepared myself for race day, following the routine that had carried me to victory time and time again throughout 2008. I prepared for Olympic gold.

However, my confidence was diminishing. My spirit shifted as a wave of guilt washed over me. Instead of releasing it, allowing it to cleanse me deep within, I held on.

As I walked out onto the track that night, there was a restlessness in my soul I couldn't tame. My sister didn't recognize me when my image appeared on the big screen. Not my usual smile, wave, and confident aura. I was broken. Instead of reaching for this finish line, I kept looking back at the line I just crossed. Prayers that typically broke through lacked any personal conviction.

I had really screwed up this time, and I knew it.

How could I ask God for this blessing when I had just done the one thing I never thought I'd do?

Finally, I'm running. Running for real. I pushed out hard and fast. Within the first 100 meters, I chased down and passed the two runners to my right and was tearing through the first straightaway.

My legs are stretched out underneath me, holding my stride, and my arms are vigorously pumping me into the next gear.

I held the lead with 100 meters still to run.

This is where I bounce, where I kick one last time and fly to the finish. This is where I leave everybody behind. They can't touch or catch me.

There's nothing between me and the line. *Keep your eyes on the finish line and just run. You can do this. Nobody knows.*

God still loves you.

Stay focused.

In the moment, San.

But there is something. And it's pulling my focus down.

The interlocking Olympic rings rise up from the track like ghosts. My past, present, and future. Instead of a clear mind focused on executing the 4 P's, my mind is cluttered, filled with doubt, shame, and unworthiness, and these are manifested in my body.

No. Oh please, God, no.

My right leg jerks stiff and straight, as if those rings leaped up and lurched onto my hamstring. I can't shift. Form is gone, poise a distant memory. My body is nothing more than a sack of bones, dragging these limbs.

All I can think about is the cramp in my hamstring. *Keep running*, I tried to tell myself.

I can't. It's gone.

The runners on the inside pull even and then surge ahead. I have no answer. Even though my hamstring remains intact, I'm in shambles. I have nothing left to give.

I'm the third one across the finish line, and gravity lowers me to my knees. My left hand covers my eyes as I try to bury myself beneath this track.

Please take this weight away from me.

In the dream the night before my race, I felt the sting of defeat, and I succumbed to it. In some weird way, I felt it was my sacrifice back to God. I didn't deserve to be on the track that day or stand on top of the podium in Beijing. I didn't feel worthy of His love.

As I composed myself to head to the podium, one of the staffers came toward me with an odd smile. He could tell I was hurting. And he wanted to say something to lift my spirits, maybe even make me laugh.

"We already had your name on the gold medal," he said, confirming the expectations of the world and affirming that I'd be waiting in vain for another four years.

I burst into tears.

Humiliation covered me. The bronze medal hung around my neck like a burden I was too broken to carry.

It was crushing in a way that can't be explained. I was so broken, physically and emotionally.

Eyes swollen by the tears, body aching from the loss, I willed myself to the medal stand. All I wanted to do was get to my family and the safe harbor of their apartment and cry. After I left the stadium, I jumped on a public bus to head away from the media, the village, and my fellow athletes. I needed a refuge, and I needed it fast.

As I boarded the bus, the loss started to sink in, and I quickly found a seat to sink into. My shoulders collapsed under the disappointment.

As the bus lurched forward, I realized I didn't know where I was. Was this even the right bus to be on?

I searched the seats for a familiar face; a trace of red, white, and blue; a Team USA hat—anything that looked familiar. Nothing. Anxiety began to suffocate me. My throat tightened, and I found it hard to breathe. A full-blown panic attack was setting in. I felt totally lost, confused, and scared. My internal warfare was now my external reality.

I got off at the next stop, weeping in agony as I tried to navigate a crowded Beijing sidewalk. It was in the midst of this foreign hysteria that a shallow "help" squeezed through the battlefield of my mind and out of my mouth as a whisper. My shaking of soul eased, and the anxiety diminished. This all-consuming peace, a peace that surpasses all understanding, flooded my heart and illuminated my spirit. I could hear the familiar, loving voice of a friend—my Father, my healer, my protector, my everything— calling out to me that it was OK, that I would be OK.

Until then, I had never truly experienced the mercy of God, had never felt His love in a physical presence. I had yet to feel Psalm 139:8: "If I go up to the heavens, you are there; if I make my bed in the depths, you are there." I didn't see that God was there with me, weeping, praying. I couldn't understand that His Son's sacrifice on the cross was *for me at my worst*.

He alone was carrying me out of my darkest time. Gentle tears fell down my cheeks as love rushed in. I felt forgiven before I even asked for it.

I found my way to my family in their rented rooms in Beijing and felt God's care, His mercy, take me there—back to a place where I knew I was loved unconditionally. We stayed up all night.

We talked and cried, and I shared with them my experience of God on the bus. They too opened up their hearts to the power of God's love that comes to us when we invite Him into our valleys.

Four days later, I was scheduled to compete in the 4x400 relay. My feelings were still raw, but enough time had passed for me to render the emotion. I heard and felt God on the street corner, and in the days that followed, I was again comfortable speaking to Him, asking for His presence and guidance. My prayers changed from confessions of guilt and pleas for mercy to expressions of gratitude and rejoicing. My God never deserted me, even in the moment I was completely lost. He never left my side. What else could I do but say thank you?

His love is *always* because of His favor and grace. I did not earn God's love; He gives it freely. And that meant I didn't have to ask Him to give it back.

I stepped onto the track without shame and brought my team from behind the Russian team to win the gold.

As a part of the Team USA 4x400 relay for five consecutive years as the anchor leg, I generally had an easy task. My teammates were strong runners who left me little work to do. Many times I ran to extend our lead and to enjoy what felt like a victory lap.

This time was different. Monique Henderson was our third leg. She started hard and strong and held a lead over our Russian competitors, but she faltered in the final 100 meters. When I took the baton, we were nearly 10 meters behind.

Stay relaxed, San. You can do this! You were born for this.

In almost the exact same position where I had allowed myself to fall apart in the 400-meter individual race, I asked God to give me the strength to bring my team the gold. Coming through the final turn, the Russian anchor leg was not budging, but in my heart, I believed it was destiny to leave Beijing with gold. In the final 20 meters of the race, I overtook my opponent and secured the victory for my team.

That 4x400 will forever be one of the most important races of my life, not because we won gold, but because it was the perfect picture of how God fights for His children. No circumstance or experience will keep God from having the victory in our lives if we let Him in.

It took time and patience for this lesson to hit my marriage.

After many years of acting like the abortion never happened, Ross and I finally sat with it. We discussed how we felt about it—raw and real—and how it had silently affected our marriage.

I always harbored some resentment toward Ross. It was our mess-up, but I felt abandoned in the decision. It was like by not saying anything, neither agreeing nor opposing, he kept his conscience clear, but it wasn't fair. We were in it together.

He explained to me that he was just as burdened by the decision as I was. He believed that our child in 2008 was a blessing we had rejected by always wanting to be in control. He knew we needed to pray together and ask for forgiveness together. We reflected on the God we know as our Savior, and that same familiar peace cloaked us like a blanket, covering doubt and giving us the grace to hope that His best for us was yet to come.

POSITION

Many times the complexities of life remind us that we are so far from our heavenly home. Life gets blurry, and we reach a crossroad where both directions feel right. Should I disobey my parents and drop out of school to pursue my passion? Should I, an aspiring politician, speak up about an issue that I know will hurt my chances of being reelected? Should I accept the promotion I feel like I've worked so hard for, even though I know my colleague is more deserving?

It takes courage to make a choice when you feel like you are in the most important phase of your race. Most times you don't know which one is right. What I know for sure is that God's love never fails and is always on the other side of your decision.

I met a young man recently who told me he was offered a track scholarship to Texas A&M, but he never went. He told me he has no idea why he didn't, but on many occasions he regrets that he didn't seize his moment, that he didn't take a chance on himself. The push and pace phases of life are important, but if you don't have the courage to make a choice when life gets tough, you might miss out on living your dream.

Chapter 10

TEAM SRR

Leading from Behind

The LORD *is my light and my salvation—*
whom shall I fear?
The LORD *is the stronghold of my life—*
of whom shall I be afraid?

PSALM 27:1

The days immediately after the Olympic race in Beijing were the first time I ever heard Mom say track was just a sport. For my family, track had always been our glue. It was our center, but in those moments, Mom was doing what she could to center our family. Dad was devastated back home in Texas, and I drifted in and out of depression. Shari couldn't even talk to God, unable to reconcile her feelings of disappointment over how God brought us this far without a victory.

It was a massive loss. Not just on the track, but in our hearts.

We were all shaken in different ways, and years went by before I could see my bronze medal as a victory.

Even with a broken spirit, I still wanted to run. Running has always been where I felt closest to God. I wanted to do what I knew God created me to do. Running is where I feel most free and full of purpose. The track has oftentimes been my church, my Bible study, my choir practice. As I've walked and jogged my "oval office" more times than I could ever count, I have created numerous hymns that flowed out of my spirit in worship.

One of my favorites, one that my sister and my cousin Yollie still sing with me to this day, goes like this:

POSITION

Speak a word, Lord,
Deep down in my spirit.
Speak a word, Lord.

I'd sing it over and over again, begging God to speak to my heart.

After Beijing, I challenged myself to start enjoying the sport again. Track and field had started from a place of love and joy. It was my great escape. The one place where I was free.

Over time, though, it changed. It was now at the center of many of my problems, and the weight of worry, doubt, fear, disappointment, expectations, and anxiety was stealing the joy out of my competition. I needed it to be fun again. I wanted to feel that sense of innocence I had enjoyed when I lined up as a kid, believing I was the fastest and wanting to prove it to myself. It was like my special talent, my poetry in motion, and I wanted it to feel that pure again.

After experiencing such devastation on the track in 2008, I questioned how I would respond. Would failure define my professional story? But by looking inward, I also lifted my gaze upward—outward—to muster the courage to pull myself together and become the champion I always knew I could be.

The 2009 season ended up being a very special year. I went undefeated in six prestigious Golden League races. I also added nine sub-50-second races to my résumé and won my first World Championships title in the 400 in Berlin.

Of all my years as a professional athlete, the 2009 season

stands out in my mind. The memories are warm and loving. On paper, 2009 is my most dominant season, but in my reflection, I don't really think about the victories; I think about the people and the journey they've traveled with me.

The love of God covered me in a way I never thought possible, and it freed me—freed from myself and from this idea that I had to be perfect. He taught me how to truly lean into and trust Him at all times.

I believe that God does work through people, and it was through trusting Him that I also sincerely embraced the people who surrounded me, sacrificed for me, and stepped up to help me pursue athletic greatness.

From my very first track meet, when my mom, dad, and sister beamed with joy as they saw me compete, I realized the unifying power of sport. Competitions were even more memorable and sweet because they always felt like family reunions or get-togethers. My entire family took time to attend my big competitions— aunts, uncles, cousins, grandparents. Some of our fondest family memories are of track meets. My sister's voice propelled me out of the blocks, but there was another voice that rivaled hers at every big completion. My Aunt Althea was always demonstrative, and I'll always remember one of my state high school meets, when I was set to race one of the fastest girls in Florida in the 4x400 relay. I had not even taken the stick, and my aunt was screaming as loud as she could. Uncle Tony, my mom's brother, insisted that she calm down, and her response became a legendary quote we still say in our family today: "Yuh nuh si mi a get emotional!"

My competitions meant something to everyone in my family, and their love and presence moved me to perform. I always joke that I had the loudest cheering section at the 2012 Olympics in London, even though defending champion Christine Ohourugu was competing just a stone's throw from where she grew up. I believe my fan section gave her a run for her money. More than thirty people traveled from all over the world to be there with me.

Professional track and field is tricky. Unlike the NFL or NBA, once you become a professional athlete, you're on your own. No built-in teammates, no collective bargaining agreements, no existing protocol. Just you, left to your own devices to create the network you need.

Relationships in this sport can either fill you or defeat you. I'm grateful to say that relationships have defined my success in track and field. I learned early on the importance of having a great supporting cast. My family taught me how to love those who sincerely invested in me, because I knew just how special it was for someone who wasn't a relative to care so deeply.

I call my select circle Team SRR, because everyone is committed to doing their part, playing their role, to help me achieve success on the track.

Bruce Johnson, my strength coach, has been a rock. He's known me since before I had a Texas driver's license. I'll never forget the first time I walked into his office at the University of Texas. Young but bold and ready to get to work as a freshman at Texas, I asked him what my program would look like for the upcoming season. As he laid it all out for me, I asked him about core work.

"How many do we do every day?"

He looked at me, perplexed. "We do a hundred or two hundred a day."

"Bruce, that is not enough," I said. "I do a thousand sit-ups every day."

I knew we'd make a great team when he said, "Well, a thousand sit-ups it is!"—much to the chagrin of my teammates. It was the start of one of my most rewarding relationships. Always holding me accountable, whether it was with core work or goal setting, Bruce became more than a coach. He's absolutely one of my best friends. Rain or snow, one-hundred-mile trip up the interstate to Waco or 9:00 p.m. workouts, he was always there, and his contribution was invaluable.

Adrik Mantingh was the other piece of the puzzle that made Team SRR a force. Originally from the Netherlands, Adrik now resides in Switzerland, and that's where I met him. He started working as my full-time physical therapist in the summer of 2007, and we ended up spending so much time together that most people had no idea he still lived in Europe. His distinct accent aside, he became as much a part of our family as anyone.

What was most amazing about Adrik is that he would train with me. No workout daunted him. He would get on the line with me and churn out eight 200-meter reps, with two minutes of rest. He would train in Zurich to stay in shape and be ready for whatever workouts I had on my plan.

As I grew older, I grew especially thankful for Adrik's willingness to suffer with me. Later in my career, following one of my surgeries, my body was slow to respond to the training. That was unusual for me, as was the daily discomfort my body was now subject to. Struggling to make my times, I was becoming discouraged. I really didn't even want to line up for my final 200, but Adrik was right there alongside me. He had run every 200 with me, and I could tell he was hurting too. That showed just how much he cared. And as I neared a breaking point when I wanted to quit, Adrik willed me off the start line and yelled, "San, you can do this. You're the best in the world. You can do this, San!" His encouragement got me to the line ahead of the time and was the turning point in my training.

After I lost in Beijing, Coach Hart urged me to start working with a sports psychologist. He had no idea the source of my true mental turmoil, but it was one of the best decisions of my career and my life. Dr. Don Corley, a Waco-based sports psychologist, became my new right-hand man.

I'll never forget our first visit.

I had been working with another doctor for about three months. He told me I put too much pressure on myself to win, and it would be a good idea to incorporate a race into my schedule for the strict purpose of training. That meant I'd run it as part of my conditioning process, and not be entirely focused on the outcome—on winning or losing. Perhaps in doing so, I could come to grips with the mounting pressure that came with almost every race. His idea was to snap the streak and win when it counted.

So at my first race of the 2009 season, I was primed to win it, but I followed his instructions, treated it more like a training run, and lost. It was the worst feeling in the world. *Why would anyone want to lose on purpose?*

I immediately made a change.

When I explained to Dr. Corley the strategy my first psychologist recommended, his expression was priceless. He remarked, "You'll never have to worry about that with me. If we're standing on the start line, you better believe our goal will always be to win."

It was the start of an amazing relationship.

Dr. Corley helped me tap into my natural inclinations to focus on the good in every situation, despite the stressors I inevitably brought to the track. He taught me to visualize success, seeing every circumstance as a step on the path toward victory.

I also loved that Dr. Corley was a Christian. Our relationship started out as one to help me achieve my goals on the track, but it quickly grew into so much more. I realized how important it was to have skilled people around me, but it was even more important to have people in my corner with strong moral pillars and convictions. I looked forward to our weekly meetings. We'd do hypnosis to visualize upcoming races, and then I'd pick his brain on his faith journey and how he overcame his personal struggles. He helped further shape my image of God as our loving, eternal Father.

With his guidance, the 2009 season ended up being a very special year. Everything was right, emotionally, spiritually, and physically.

And the best part was my dad finally started traveling the circuit with me for the first time in my career. He still thinks he was my good-luck charm, but I like to think the combination of Dr. Corley's support and his presence made the difference.

For my efforts during the 2009 season, I was awarded the IAAF Female Athlete of the Year for the second time in my career. At the awards banquet, Prince Albert of Monaco presented me the trophy. It was so heavy that I handed it back to him and asked if he'd hold it while I gave my speech. I returned to my seat, to the snickers of my dad. "Only *you* would think it's OK to ask a prince to hold your trophy."

Dad loved when I was like that, just being myself.

It was a memorable season because I exchanged the humiliation of 2008 into humility. The track reveals my every truth. Between those lines, in the lane, under the glare of the spotlight, I can't hide. The source of one of my greatest blessings—the gift to run—also confronts me with significant weaknesses.

It's tricky because the world grooms us to be competitive. To look for every edge and angle to gain advantage over a rival. Winning isn't everything; it's the *only* thing. Whatever it takes. Second place sucks. These are the motivational idioms of our time, but they tend to push us to diminish the character of our peers instead of asking more of ourselves.

I projected all my hurt emotions onto the competitors lining up next to me on the track.

Not only did God soften my heart, but in my journey to deal with certain inner demons, He used the track to teach me about life's Golden Rule—to do to others what I would have them do to me, to love my neighbor as myself. On that track, it meant loving my competitors.

As I stood atop the podium to accept my World Championships individual title in 2009, a moment I'd dreamed about my entire life, my heart and mind were filled with other images. It was surreal. I couldn't wait to get back on the track and run in the 4x400 relay with my teammates.

Team USA is typically favored to win, and that's especially true in the 4x400 relay. The United States is blessed with a gifted pool of quarter-milers, and with depth and experience, we are always a force.

Energy overwhelms me as I walk into a buzzing stadium, wearing red, white, and blue, flanked by three powerful teammates. I imagine the rush of adrenaline that Superman must have felt when he donned his cape and flew out of the telephone booth, and surely it matches what Team USA experiences as we walk, shoulder to shoulder, toward the start line. Invincible.

That day in Berlin, we took a commanding lead from the very first lap and won the relay by more than four seconds. We ran one of the top-five fastest times in history.

I thanked God for giving me the time to see the point I was missing all along: my gift of running was meant to simply give me a stage to show people how good God is, and I believe that God's love is best observed, best modeled, when we reach out and embrace those around us.

It was a lesson I learned the hard way, through the way I had previously become fixated, nearly obsessed, with beating my opponents and how I had also been subjected to bitter, vain treatment.

In 2004, when I decided to become a professional athlete, getting an agent was the first task. At the time, I thought I would continue training with Coach Kearney, and she told me there were only two people she would work with. I met with both and opted to work with Renaldo Nehemiah.

He was a world-class hurdler and world-record holder at one time. He came well dressed, with an impressive presentation. He was convincing, and as a young teenager on the brink of a pro career, I looked forward to his mentorship. I knew what I wanted to accomplish in the sport and the importance of having great people around me. I was optimistic that our relationship would be long-term and successful.

Once the season got underway, I realized he was not the mentor and teacher I had hoped for and that it did not look like it was going to work out in the end. He didn't check in on my progress, rarely attended my competitions, and on the whole just didn't give me the time and attention I had received from my coaches and thought I deserved.

On one occasion, I called him about prize money I had earned. I'll never forget his response.

"Didn't I just pay you? What do you need money for so soon?"

I was shocked. It was my money, and he had no right to keep

it from me or question why I wanted it. Thankfully he did send me the money in the end.

Based on the rules of our governing body, the IAAF, an agent can't sign an athlete for more than one year, so as soon as the year was up, I terminated my contract and hired my mom and dad to be my full-time agents.

Renaldo had negotiated my Nike contract for four years. My initial deal ran from 2004 to 2008. I ended my working relationship with Renaldo in 2005. In 2006, having completed a full year of working with my parents, we renegotiated the contract with Nike. I was so happy. I was now one of the highest-paid female sprinters, had a wonderful working relationship with everyone on my team, and continued to pay Renaldo his fees from the original contract until 2008.

Renaldo's agency took the payments and then sued me for more.

I couldn't believe it. I was devastated. How could a star athlete, who knew just how hard it is to save that kind of money in our sport, do this to me?

At nineteen years old, I signed an agreement that tied his agency to my Nike contract in perpetuity. Of course, I had no idea what it meant and felt I had done my due diligence when I asked our trusted lawyer to look over it and give it his stamp of approval.

I fought hard, went to an arbitrator, and pleaded my case.

I paid taxes, agent fees, housing expenses in Waco, and coaching fees, as well as tithing on a regular basis. Many times, I only took home 25 to 30 percent of what I generated. I understood the law, but hoped the arbitrator would find a compromise that was fair.

Renaldo Nehemiah walked into a team room on the University of Texas campus, after a lifetime's worth of training and sacrifice by my family and myself, worked for one year, and was entitled to almost $300,000 of my earnings?

How could that be right?

When the arbitrator came back with the ruling, my heart sank. It was a tough way for a young professional to learn a lesson. I think that relationship scarred me to a point where I was skeptical to really let people in, which is why the turning point in 2009 was significant. I broke down those walls and let the Lord take over, and He showed me the truly good people I had around me. Their love and loyalty stood out.

I try to always keep my eyes forward and my head up, and by looking ahead, it's easier to see good. I challenged myself to make something positive out of a negative situation, and a positive that came from my relationship with Renaldo was my partnership with my first major sponsor. A company world-renowned for supporting and building the brands and stories for athletes in every sport, Nike has a reputation that needs little introduction. In the sports world, it stands alone.

As my career grew, I became more and more connected to the financial support and emotional connection of this brand. From billboards to training shoes, Nike has given me some of the greatest shine a young girl from Kingston could have ever hoped for. I worked with the best in the business. Not only valued as an athlete, I felt like part of the team. They've invited me to meet with innovators to provide input for spikes and racing kits and allowed me to tour the world as an ambassador. Nike was and continues to be my sports family.

The track, where I am most driven and consumed with competitive desire, is actually the one place that truly taught me to love my neighbor as myself.

The reality of the sport I love is that it requires a tremendous amount of financial support to compete at an elite level. Literally it takes a team of people around me to make my success possible, day in and day out. These professionals have dedicated their entire lives to support a single aspect of my career. Take Adrik, for example, who traveled to stay with me in Texas for weeks at a time and accompany me to all my competitions. Without his expert hands, my sore and aching muscles would have never recovered at the rate necessary to compete in events around the globe. He spent time with me to understand the unique intricacies of how my body responds to training, traveling, and the tactical components of my stride.

At the center of all these professions is the athlete—me. My production on the track is what financially enables these professionals to also do what they love. I see it as a blessing to be a blessing—that by using my gift and succeeding in my sport, I am able to help others realize their dreams.

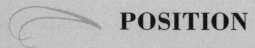

POSITION

What I learned from the track, the place where I am most driven and consumed with competitive desire, is actually how to love my neighbor as myself.

It's important to win and to give your best, but not at the cost of missing out on the joy that comes when you open your heart and develop the relationships around you.

In the end, it won't be the medals or the promotions that mean the most; it will be the people and the memories you create along the way.

Empower others to be their best and to lead from behind. You operate best when you aren't trying to fill every role yourself but trusting the people on your team to do their part.

God wants us to love each other, to lean on each other, and to make each other better.

Chapter 11

GLAM & GOLD

Leaping on Faith

*"Therefore I tell you, do not worry about your life,
what you will eat or drink; or about your body,
what you will wear. Is not life more than food, and
the body more than clothes? Look at the birds of
the air; they do not sow or reap or store away in
barns, and yet your heavenly Father feeds them.
Are you not much more valuable than they?"*

MATTHEW 6:25–26

One of the things that Dr. Corley had challenged me to do was explore new opportunities off the track. He taught me that to run the best races of my life, I needed to realize that racing couldn't be my entire life. I had to allow myself to find new projects and follow new passions. In order to enhance my focus on the track, I began to widen my horizon. If the track was all I had, I'd hold it too closely, and that wasn't healthy. I experienced that in Beijing.

My family's bond has always been a thing of fascination for people when they meet us. I started dreaming about creating our own family reality show. I thought we had all the components for a hit television series.

Ross and I were discovering new joy as newlyweds; my sister and I had just opened our own hair salon; Mom and Dad were quite the characters acting as my parents and managers; and my cousin Yollie was doing all my media outreach and styling.

I plotted out story lines and scripted out all the characters. What started as some doodling in a notebook grew into a forty-slide PowerPoint presentation. Through my management at Creative Artists Agency (CAA), I was connected to Katie Maloney, an unscripted TV agent. She appreciated the work I had put into the concept of my show and worked diligently to orchestrate meetings with different networks

The process wasn't quick—it lasted about four years from concept to development, actually going from boardroom to boardroom and presenting the concept to talent agents for different networks. Sometimes I went alone, talking through my ideas, but Katie suggested that Mom and Yollie accompany me so the networks could see the reality of our relational dynamic.

Yollie and Mom were in the room for the presentation with WeTv, the network that eventually agreed to produce the show.

I was over the moon. I had admired Rev. Run's family show *Run's House* for so long and wanted to be the "Jamerican" version of that. Angela Simmons, daughter of the legendary Rev. Run from the hip-hop group Run DMC, and I were just quickly becoming friends, and she gave me the contact to her production company.

As a family, we were always a team, but this would be different. It was no longer all of us working together behind the scenes and me representing us on the field.

On the show, we'd all stand together in front of the camera.

But the reality of reality TV wasn't exactly what I expected. When your show has finally been given the green light, it takes anywhere from six to nine months before you ever film. The story lines you sell are real and organic then, but half a year later, they're old and a distant memory. It was hard to go back and deliver on story lines that were no longer our reality.

For instance, my sister and her now-husband Tyrell had just started dating. Tyrell was one of Ross's best friends from college. The beginning of Shari and Tyrell's relationship was rocky. Shari felt Tyrell was "the one" from early on in their relationship (like most girls do, in my opinion), but he wasn't so convinced. They had great moments, but they also had epic fights and breakups that made both Ross and me question the stability of their relationship.

About four weeks before we started filming for our new show, Shari and Tyrell had one of their worst fights. It started over the simplest thing. My sister is a huge Beyoncé fan and would never miss a performance or television appearance. So the minute it was announced that Beyoncé was doing the halftime show at the Super Bowl, we couldn't wait.

Ross and I hosted a small watch party. Nichole, my best friend, and her husband, Tevin, joined us as well. I couldn't tell you which two teams were playing—when Ross wasn't on the field, it didn't mean as much to me. For my sister and me, it was the Beyoncé Bowl, and we were watching, front and center.

Tyrell was just getting to know Shari, but upon meeting my sister you know two things: don't mess with her hair, and don't talk about Beyoncé. I don't remember exactly what Tyrell said, but it turned into a war of words like I'd never heard before.

As he went on and on about Beyoncé's performances always being the same, Shari put her fingers in her ears and began to hum over his comments.

"You're so childish."

"I could never marry someone like you!"

Shari was crushed.

She fired back as we began to get up, "You'll never have to worry about that!"

Shari was in tears, devastated by how quickly a small argument had escalated to a full-blown fight. My show producers and I were in constant communication up to this point—talking every day or so, crafting story lines. I told them what had transpired between Shari and Tyrell.

However, by the time we started filming, Shari and Tyrell were doing much better. They had worked through their early-stage woes and were getting into fewer arguments and building a stronger bond.

Once the producers were in town, they wanted to see the old Shari and Tyrell we had sold months before we started filming. Ironically, when something is behind you, you don't realize how easy it is to oversell it. In many of the scenes with Shari and Tyrell, in an effort to meet and in some ways exceed everyone's expectations of him, Tyrell oversold his character.

There were so few scenes that showed their infatuation with each other, and that was a mistake.

We had many regrets over how we were portrayed in our first time on TV. There were glimmers of our real personalities, but we never got in a groove or had an opportunity to fully be ourselves.

It was disappointing. My hope all along was to show a loving family that inevitably had conflicts and issues but always overcame them with integrity, humor, and love.

I never felt we were forced to do anything. Like many projects, sometimes it just gets off track, and you can't reel it back in.

There were other moments of give-and-take that changed the scope of my original project. I wanted to call the show

Running Things—a woman running things on the track and in the workplace—but the producers liked *Glam & Gold*.

After the first episode, a new producer joined the team. He wanted more drama, more conflict, and more jaw-dropping moments. After filming the third episode, I wanted to push back. I wanted to go back to my original vision, but I didn't trust my instincts.

It was disappointing when the final product wasn't what I foresaw, and the show wasn't renewed for a second season.

I'm content with trying and failing, a lesson I learned over and over on the track, but this failure felt different. I was the first track and field athlete to walk into a room with high-level executives and win herself a reality TV show. I was confident and poised, and they liked that. They saw the potential in me. But midway through the project, I let fear and doubt creep in.

Maybe they know better, I told myself. *Maybe we* do *need more drama, more action.*

I allowed myself to be swayed by others' opinions when I should have been more grounded in my own convictions. It felt like when I lost the World Championships race to Tonique. I was disappointed because I moved away from my inner guidance. I didn't trust the power of my own vision.

God's delay was actually my blessing. If the show had continued for another season, my family would have continued to be misrepresented and the lightheartedness of our dysfunction misconstrued for the value of ratings.

Although the landscape of reality TV keeps evolving, with

more and more outlandish and unbelievable story lines and characters, I know it's important to have positive shows, especially in the black community, and I hope at the right time we'll be given an opportunity again.

POSITION

I believe it's OK to ask God why you find yourself in a particular circumstance. But you have to be ready to hear His answer.

Many times we want something so badly, and God in His infinite wisdom allows us to see whether it's good or bad for us. Some blessings in life blossom outside of their season, but the journey always equips us with knowledge if we allow ourselves to be open and learn along the way.

It's important to try new things—to go for it. But always know that God ultimately has the final say and always knows what's best.

POISE

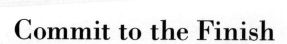

Commit to the Finish

Chapter 12

LEAN IN

Trusting the Plan

*Those who hope in the LORD will
  renew their strength.
  They will soar on wings like eagles;
they will run and not grow weary,
  they will walk and not be faint.*

ISAIAH 40:31

I hold a special fondness for the track at Hayward Field. It's filled with amazing historical moments, a place where legends are born. I was hoping this audience would see me do something great.

The Prefontaine Classic is competed annually, and in an Olympic year, it is America's marquee tune-up race. Hayward Field is home to both the Classic and the Olympic Trials, which were set for the last week of June. "The Pre" in 2012 felt like a practice for the trials, because all the big names were there.

The stadium was electric with anticipation. The community of Eugene, which is home to a huge tribe of runners, embraces track and field. More than mere spectators in the stadium, these are knowledgeable, informed runners who scan the horizon to witness what most believe is impossible.

On race day, I was happy for the presence of my family and their easy conversation at breakfast. It was a very calm start to the day, which is nice, because from there, everything accelerated.

Seeing Dad on the track that day gave me a calm sense of comfort, like I was going into battle with a friend. As I jogged, stretched, got a massage, and progressed through my drills, I reflected on just how blessed I was to always have him in my corner.

I can only imagine the caliber of athlete my dad would have

been had he received even an ounce of the gentle nurturing and guidance he poured into me. Family members and friends tell me he was a natural on the soccer field. In Jamaica, I'm better known as Archie's daughter than as an Olympic champion.

Because there were few recordings when my father played, I have had to enjoy his talent as told through the many fans who enjoyed his legendary ability to dribble past his competitors and cause them to fall off balance, his innate ability to score corner kicks, and his swag and charisma on the field. My mom mostly recalls that. Dad represented his country on the Under-19 national junior team.

Unfortunately, his family did not understand the sports landscape or provide the support he needed to continue to reach his full potential. One of the few pointers Dad did receive was to not lift weights. Strength training was presumed to hinder speed. This is a statement I can testify is completely false, yet as a young man, Dad had no way of knowing that. So he eventually moved on, settling on soccer and sports as just hobbies and vowing that if he ever had children with athletic talent, he would fight to not only protect it, but also promote it.

My dad helped me find my competitive voice. With him by my side, I was able to discover myself. I found my passion and talent, not because he showed it to me, but because he led me to it.

I felt courageous and powerful that day. I wasn't just competing to fulfill my dreams and destiny; I was furthering his journey as well.

Checking in for my race, I said one more prayer with my family and headed to the contentious call room for some final preparations. As I walked out to lane 4 that day, on the track where I felt at home, everything about my day had gone according to plan. From the time I woke up to the music I played, I had perfectly controlled everything within my power.

Despite all my preparation, I started to doubt myself.

I began to question my ability.

Looking back, I think it's interesting that when I appeared most invincible, the Lord allowed me to feel my own humanity and weakness.

My racing season had started in the dead of winter with a full indoor schedule, and heading into March, I had won my first World Indoor title in Istanbul, Turkey. Indoor racing is different—the track is banked and a shorter distance—but the victory gave me a lot of confidence going into the outdoor part of my schedule.

My first big outdoor race had taken place at the Jamaica Invitational at the National Stadium in Kingston. I'm always motivated to run well when I return to Jamaica, and despite running for America, it always feels like I have a home track advantage because of the number of family and friends in the stands. Plus, I was full of fire coming off my World Indoor championship and eager to translate that indoor win to an outdoor victory, but Jamaican Novlene Williams-Mills ran 49.9, a very fast race for early May, and nipped me at the line to win.

The defeat in Jamaica left me questioning my form and strategy.

Confidence requires balance, and it's a razor-thin line where pride meets humility. Before many of my races, these two seem to face off.

Standing in lane 4 at Hayward back in Eugene, just two weeks after the loss in Jamaica, with Novlene to my right in lane five, my focus centered on silencing the monkey chatter bouncing around my brain. Athletes think of those opposing voices, the negative thoughts, the loud whispers of doubt, as mental monkey chatter. It's nonsense, meaningless—but it can haunt you. And around my starting blocks, the monkey chatter was beginning to drown out what I knew to be true: I could win this race.

Instead of reinforcing what could go right, I was assessing all the things that might go wrong.

And to top it all off, the wind began gusting inside the stadium. I actually chuckled to myself as the weather began to manifest my inward struggle. *This can't be happening*, I thought as I searched for something that was going my way. I settled for thinking at least I braided my hair so it wouldn't get in my eyes.

Taking a deep breath and closing my eyes, I realized that my hair was a point to be thankful for. With the confidence of a daughter whose Father was truly watching, I whispered, "Peace! Be still!"

What happened instead was greater than I could have ever imagined.

The winds in the stadium ceased.

Kneeling down, I settled into my blocks, knowing that whatever the outcome, I was running that day not against anyone but *with* the One.

Novlene, who was in lane 5, and Amantle Montsho, who was inside me in lane 3, are both very aggressive runners. After the first 100 meters, they usually like to hit the gas. Compared to them, I try to be conservative on the backstretch. With this approach, I typically have enough fuel in my tank to stay poised and kick through the finish.

When we came through the last turn, Amantle was out in front by a few meters, and Novlene and I were dead even. I said to myself, *Don't panic.* It was like I inhaled an extra breath. My muscles weren't tense or tight. I wasn't overthinking. I was free from any negative thoughts. I was free to run and free from doubt, and my body knew it. I worked my arms to help generate a last kick and pulled away through the tape.

I punched the air with my right arm as I crossed the line. The fight was over, and I had won. It was an important win on a big stage, and I felt triumphant in that moment. Within seconds, a new feeling washed over me. I started shaking my fists in front of me like a giddy little kid. *This is what it feels like*, I thought to myself, and I thanked God for showing me the way to victory and sharing the moment with me.

It was scary, though. Trusting God's will for my life didn't ensure that I would never face hardship or that I would never lose another race. The promise was not that I would have painless short-term wins. In fact, it practically assured me I would face trials and tribulations, but I was strengthened by believing that God's plan for me was far better than anything I could ever dream of or imagine.

I found freedom in that obedience. It didn't relieve me from the daily work—from the struggle and sacrifice of training and racing—but I was set free from the trivial worry of not measuring up, of not being good enough. This new approach silenced the "what ifs" in my life, and I imagine it's the same seed of faith that motivated Dad as a younger man. Although he felt the call as a competitive athlete, the setting and circumstances of his life didn't promote it.

Instead of forcing the issue, he was satisfied to wait. My father was satisfied to treasure my triumphs as greater than his own.

When I came through the final turn at the Prefontaine, I was trailing in the race, but I wasn't afraid. Nothing negative held me back. I continued to work the strategy of the race, knowing the Lord was also working.

He isn't about to abandon His work.

POISE

We all have the power to move mountains in our lives with a word, but it first starts with belief.

Do the work and remain prayerful. Stay the course, and stay poised through the finish.

In the midst of our striving, preparing as best we can, controlling what we can, we still have to accept our powerlessness against certain forces. We have to completely surrender ourselves to trusting God, that He will direct our path and lead us into His will for our lives.

Chapter 13

EXCHANGE ZONE

Accepting Change

*But if we hope for what we do not yet
have, we wait for it patiently.*

ROMANS 8:25

Relays, to me, are the most elegant and most graceful events to observe in the sport of track and field. As four runners blend their unique talents to compete in unison, a successful relay is not only a harmony of speed but also a rhythm of reaction.

The baton is the key, and it must be played correctly. When everything works in the right step, you almost don't see the stick as it's handed off. The exchange just happens, like a natural flow of motion. But the handoff is actually a practiced dance. A runner's steps have to be in accord with the other's. If you're out of sync, if you're stepping out of turn, you'll miss the moment for the exchange.

Timing is everything.

In Beijing at the 2008 Olympic Games, Team USA's 4x100m relay team was disqualified for not passing the baton during the 20-meter exchange zone. I watched with eager anticipation, because Lauryn Williams, one of my best friends, was running the anchor leg. Even as a bystander, I observed the race as a runner—timing their steps, counting strides, and reading faces like I was prepared to accept the stick and continue the race.

Lauryn was awaiting Tori Edwards for the final exchange of the relay. She took off, but after some hesitancy and confusion, they dropped the stick. They were both prepared and primed to make the perfect exchange, but they missed the window and the opportunity to win gold.

It was heartbreaking to witness my teammates with their heads hung low as they walked off the track in disappointment, but it's even harder to witness someone miss their window of opportunity in their everyday life.

Transition in life is much like the way I see a well-executed relay.

One toe. One tiny toe. Actually, it's my right big toe, but in comparison to the rest of my body—to the other muscles and tendons and bones I call on and pound on to motor around a track—the toe is quite small. But don't tell that to my right big toe. You might hurt its feelings.

My toe first started talking to me as a junior in high school. *Slow down*, it said. And I almost cried out—the pain was so intense. I told the toe to be quiet, and I kept running. We've had a contentious relationship ever since.

Since I was seven years old, I've asked a lot of that toe. I've dug that toe tight against the turf, coiled my whole body weight on top of it, and pressed into it to begin the push phase of my race. I can't be mad at it. Thousands of times, probably hundreds of thousands of times, those itty-bitty bones, barely worth measuring in inches, have absorbed the weight of my existence and projected me forward.

My toe eventually broke. I broke it. I don't remember exactly when—shocking, I know—and the when doesn't matter as much as the why. I worked it, worked it, and worked it some more. The toe didn't splinter or shatter; it just cracked a little, to prove a point.

You're not perfect, Sanya, it told me. *You won't last forever.*

I didn't need the X-ray to see it; I could feel it. The rigid, stiff thunderbolt that shot up through my foot and leg every time I put my weight on it spoke pretty clearly.

By the time I crossed the finish line to win the 4x400m relay and second gold medal in London, I couldn't ignore the toe any longer. Surgery was a necessity. Not to fix it, but to join the bones together with a few screws so it could withstand more years of digging and pushing. My toe told me it would keep trying, but it also told me it was time to mentally and spiritually prepare myself for what was next.

My toe inspired my instinct, my constant reminder, that I inevitably would go through an exchange zone in my life.

Surgery to repair the bones in my toe was never promised as a fix-all. I knew that running or racing pain-free wasn't in the cards anymore, but as athletes, pain is a common training partner. I think we actually embrace it as a sensation that tells us we're alive and working. We hold it close, toughening our resolve because of its very existence. It gives us a mental edge. I would tell myself, *If this is hurting me, it must be killing my competitors.*

I had the procedure on my toe late in 2012, and it required a couple months of rehabilitation. The expectation was that I could start training again in February 2013. That gave me a bit of a late start, but coming off an Olympic year, I didn't mind the prospect of missing the indoor season. I'd be ready to go by summer, when the European Diamond League races are in full swing.

The toe had other ideas. I'd had pain before, but after the surgery, it felt like I lost all the flexion in the joint. Not only could I not stand to put my weight into it, but the foot was too rigid and stiff to allow me to lift into my stride. It was worse than before.

Training was abbreviated at best. When I'm in season, it's a five-days-a-week job, from morning to night. I'm in the weight room first thing, then rehab and recovery, and then track and core work in the evening. But the pain and lack of flexibility made it difficult to string together more than a couple days of training in a row.

I always believed in my ability to compete when it matters. So against Coach Hart's recommendation, I competed at the USATF National Championships in June 2013. The pain was so severe that I ran the finals of the 400 in my sneakers. Everyone joked that I must have the record out of lane 2 in sneakers, not our usual racing spikes, finishing sixth in 51.9 seconds.

We decided on another surgery to smooth down the bones, which we hoped would help me run more comfortably. It was the best course of action, but it also meant I'd be out of work for the summer of 2013.

Here I was, coming face-to-face with the reality that I would have to begin to imagine life outside of my "oval office." Now with no racing schedule to focus on, it was time to consider my other passions and competencies as avenues for me to contribute to the world in new ways.

I needed to prepare for my transition.

The tough thing about this next phase was that it would move me into completely unfamiliar territory. My entire life was shaped around the idea of winning races. I never had a part-time job, never pursued summer internships, never even considered what kind of professional I'd be if I weren't a professional athlete. But by winning these races, I had access to a network I could tap into. I just had to open my heart to the idea of using it.

During the course of my career, I've had the opportunity to meet some of the brightest and most inspirational industry leaders—breakfast with Bob Costas, discussing how he made his indelible mark in broadcasting; lunch with Mark Parker, the CEO of Nike; and dinner with Kevin Liles, music mogul and former president of Def Jam Recordings.

Every meeting was special and unforgettable. During this unique time of awareness as I readied for transition, Kevin Liles made a huge impact on my thought process. He challenged me to articulate what the SRR brand meant, what I stood for, and what personal pillars others could connect to. He admired everything I did on the track but explained the importance of branding, of setting myself apart by defining who I was.

From that moment on, I worked hard to develop the SRR brand. He told me to think of three words that companies and individuals could relate to and then to be sure everything I did aligned with my core values. The three words I selected were *excellence, philanthropy*, and *beauty*.

After 2012, my off-seasons weren't true off-periods any longer.

I knew I was racing toward the exchange zone of my career. I had to prepare. I had to make decisions and sacrifices to build my brand. Many times there was no pay, just the pursuit of an opportunity. It was tiresome at times, and it felt like work, because I was juggling two selves—Sanya, the defending Olympic champion, and Sanya, the fashionista, entrepreneur, philanthropist, and aspiring media personality.

Some days I lamented the loss of innocence and longed for the days at Vaz Prep, when I was so excited by the discovery of my talent and the process of developing it. There were no decisions then, no worries or struggles, but just the joy of work.

And I realized that the new blessing I searched for was no different. The blessing was the opportunity. The reward wouldn't be a tangible thing any longer—no more medals and trophies—but a chance to continue the journey, to experience new people and places. Yes, that would be work, but to work is to be blessed.

After my third surgery in 2015, I knew that had to be my last. My toe had given me so much, and it was time to finally give it the rest it deserved. The 2016 track season would be my final one, no matter the outcome.

It was time to enter my exchange zone.

When I officially announced my retirement at the start of the 2016 season, I felt vulnerable and a little lost. Yes, in my heart I knew it was time, but it took every ounce of courage and faith I had to actually do it. I prepared my post for social media two weeks prior to actually making it public. Thoughts kept filling my head. *Maybe the toe will calm down again. Maybe God isn't through with me on the track.*

But I knew it was time to let it go.

I had given twenty-four of my thirty-one years to my sport and had been rewarded greatly. And even though it caused me great pain every day, I still loved it. I knew there was still more running in my legs. But I realized in the moments leading up to my retirement announcement that it was time to show my appreciation for my gift by returning it to the Giver and stepping out in the faith that what He had in store for me would be even greater.

The beauty and brilliance of God's plans are all around us—if only we take the time to be self-aware and look. Days after my final race, I received a call from the producers at NBC. They wanted me to join their team in the broadcasting booth for the remainder of the Olympic Trials and for the upcoming Olympic Games in Rio.

Within a week of really, fully laying down my crown, the adventure in broadcasting began. My courage in announcing my retirement and letting go of my first love paid off. What might have not happened until several years later, had I gotten my way, became a sudden promotion into a lifelong dream that is just beginning.

Faith and courage get us safely through the exchange zone. No two handoffs are alike. But we always want the same outcome: to achieve the passing of the baton and to keep running. Just taking the next step, I realized, is an act of hope as you trust God to see you through.

POISE

Fear seems to work in one of two ways: it either pushes you into unsafe waters or traps you into panic.

Fear prevents us from entering the next stage of success. Instead of keeping our heads down and trusting the process—trusting our preparation and practice—we get jumpy and move on too quickly. Other times we are afraid to move. When the window opens for us to transition through the exchange zone of life, we hold too tightly to our comfort zones, our proven gifts, our past successes.

Fear holds us back from embracing every season of our lives, which are richly rewarded when we pursue those exchanges with God as our running companion. We must be present and have the courage to step out in faith when we know it's time to move on and accept the plans that our Father has laid out for us.

Chapter 14

VICTORY LAP

Taking a Bow

*[Jesus said,] "I have told you these things, so that in me
you may have peace. In this world, you will have trouble.
But take heart! I have overcome the world."*

JOHN 16:33

S ome victory laps are in the perfect shape of an oval, a track; others look more like a figure eight. I've experienced both.

The Call
Friday, July 1, 2016

Be still.

I heard my words, and the voice that speaks to me so clearly on this track. I realized He was talking to me.

Walk the Talk
July 2012

The minute I stepped into the athletes' village at the 2012 London Games, I was the Olympic champion. I walked and talked as if I had already won. I kept repeating to myself, *I am the champ.*

In my preparation for my third Olympics, I incorporated intense visualization. I had already seen myself winning. I already knew what I would do when I crossed the finish line. Everything unfolded as if I was executing a plan I had rehearsed hundreds of times in my mind.

Pops and Me
July 2016

When I arrived in Eugene, Oregon, in July for the 2016 Olympic Trials, I knew it would be my final time competing at historic Hayward Field. Some of my proudest professional moments in the sport of track and field have happened here, and it felt right that I would compete to represent Team USA a fourth time in Olympic competition on this track.

Since winning my first individual gold medal at the 2012 London Olympics, injuries slowed me down. First, it was a busted right toe, finally cracking after years of hard training and racing, and then just weeks before the trials, I pulled my hamstring in a tune-up meet.

I had barely run in the days leading up to trials, let alone sprinted. Part of me knew my heart was making promises my body wasn't able to deliver, but my entire career had been built on my ability to look forward, eyes up and head up, hopeful in the pursuit. When we finished the workout the day before my first qualifying heat, Dad was by my side. I looked at him in the twilight and thought how perfect everything was. When it came to race strategy and planning, Dad is my ace, my go-to, my steady. I was thirty-one now, and we started just like this when I was seven—Dad and me shutting down the track, heading home in the last moments of sunlight.

"Let's take a walk," I said to him.

We walked the oval, and he pointed out specific parts of the track and what he remembered about them. Normally, we'd be going over the race, visualizing how I would run, but this time Dad and I talked about how far we'd come and what a blessing it was to be here. Dad told me how proud he was of me.

Pre-race Meeting
August 2012

The 2012 Olympic Final fell on a Sunday. That morning, I woke up rested and surrounded by my family. I chose to stay with them in a London rented house instead of in the village. Honestly, I don't think Shari would have allowed it any other way. She was still scarred from my sleepless, strung-out, alien behavior in Beijing. Around family, we are able to charge each other's spirits. It reinforced our confidence, and we controlled the energy evenly. I had at least thirty friends and family who traveled across the Atlantic for the race, but visitors were managed thoughtfully.

The morning of the race, Pastor Gaylon Clark, who leads the ministry at my church in Austin, Greater Mount Zion, came by our rented house. What began as a normal conversation with me and my family grew into a devotional, our own special sermon. It was perhaps the only part of the London experience I didn't imagine or plan in advance. I had promised myself that I'd manage my emotions as much as I could, keep as much as I could for the race, but I allowed myself to experience God that morning on the couch with Ross, Mom, Dad, sister, and aunt. I let the tears flow as I felt God moving in the room. Pastor Clark reminded me that

I was running in the race of my life, but it wasn't on the track. My crown was in heaven.

After I dressed and readied my hair and face and left to get on the bus for the stadium, Shari turned to Ross and my parents.

"This is it," she said. "This is definitely it."

Head Up, Eyes Forward
July 2016

The day of my final race, I was optimistic. I was excited. I realized I was taking a big chance. That I was risking a lot. There was the issue of my health and my pulled hamstring, which hadn't had the full six weeks it truly required to heal, and there was also the possibility of epic embarrassment. I could be lining myself up to fail, but I saw this race as an opportunity for my greatest comeback.

Like he did for all my races, Coach Hart scribbled the timeline of our warm-up routine on a tiny sheet of paper. Every drill was scripted to the minute, and even though I had every fifteen-minute increment memorized, I still found comfort in seeing his handwriting.

I struggled to get through my 30–60–90 meter progressions. I had the power to burst, but not the strength to shift. Coach Hart told me it might not be a good idea to actually line up and run. Could my leg hold up under the shifting of speed that is required to race a full quarter mile around the track?

"Coach," I said, "I didn't come all this way not to try."

Focus
August 2012

Everything develops a little slower at the Olympics. They call everyone back to the ready room almost an hour before the race starts, because TV dictates the timing, so we're all just jogging around, trying to keep our muscles warm and loose and our focus locked and in the zone.

I thought through my strategy and anticipated what to expect in the race. Coach Hart gave me one last reminder. He told me the Russian runner on my inside starts races like a madwoman.

"She's going to come up on you and pass you," he said. "That's OK. Let her go. She won't be able to hold it."

Finally we checked in and got our hip numbers. Mine weren't sticking to my uniform because it was so hot. *Oh no. Heat.* I drifted back to Beijing. An outside thought. A distraction. I quickly slapped it out of sight, out of mind.

Final Lap
July 2016

The first time I raced at Hayward Field as a teenager, I finished second, and they let me take a half victory lap. The announcer said the fans wanted to keep on cheering me, and it was a good opportunity to introduce myself to them. Every chance I got, I came back and raced on that track, because everyone had welcomed me and embraced me, when all I had given them was the promise for more.

In the thirteen years since, I worked to earnestly fulfill that promise, and I stood on the track in 2016 as the aging champion, chasing not promise but progress. America's next promising talent was just a few lanes to my right. Only a few weeks before, Courtney Okolo completed a championship career at the University of Texas, where she broke most of my 400 records.

What were the chances?

Dream It. See It. Do It.
August 2012

When the camera panned in on me in lane 6 of London's Olympic Stadium, I made sure to smile and blow a kiss into the camera. Hold my arms up and wave to my front, and wave behind me. Just like I had practiced.

I kept fumbling with my hip numbers, trying to smack them into sticking despite the hot temperatures. I was in my own little world, until the stadium erupted when they announced Christine Ohuruogu, the British defending Olympic champion. Her native country's support was loud and demonstrative. I wasn't anticipating that.

OK, San, just relax. Breathe. Get back in your zone.

I didn't plan for the crowd noise, but Dr. Corley and I *did* plan for distraction. It would just be a source of motivation to fuel me forward in the process. As my breathing slowed down, I absorbed the energy and eased back into the intensity of the moment.

What I love about the Olympics, once you get into the blocks, it's like the whole stadium goes in with you. Everyone is silent and focused. And then, boom.

"LET'S GO, SANYA!"

Shifting Speeds
July 2016

The race started like every race of my life. The gun goes, and I push out of the blocks. I charge out as hard as I can, but when I got to the backstretch, I knew I was running a different race. My stride couldn't open, and my legs refused to stretch out underneath me. When it was time to make the turn and really go, I had nothing. The field was moving away from me, and I couldn't chase them.

When everything in my being wanted to push forward, to fly down the homestretch of the track one more time, cross the line first one more time, I stopped.

Sanya, be still.

And I stopped running.

First, Finally
August 2012

I charged out hard and found a comfortable pace. About 200 meters into the race, the blonde Russian runner passed me on the left. *That's a good thing*, I told myself. Just like Coach Hart said.

At the top of the last turn, all I could think was position, position, position. I didn't want to give it too much gas and then tie up at the end. Into the last straightaway, I felt American DeeDee Trotter in my peripheral. She pulled ahead.

No way. She is not beating me. I worked my arms and asked my legs for one more kick. That gave me enough to get in front of her. *Hold on, just hold on and get to the line. Keep your eyes on the line.* I dipped my left shoulder, reached out with my right arm, and prayed.

That was it. I finished first.

I was the champ.

A Distinct Voice
July 2016

For a moment, I hung my head. This is not the way it was supposed to end.

Then I heard a voice, this time a woman's voice, high in the stands above the track. "We love you, Sanya," she called to me. It snapped me into the present moment, and I lifted my eyes up. There was no exit, no way for me to escape, and so I walked. I walked toward the finish line.

And would you believe it? The fans stood and cheered. To tell you the truth, it felt just like when they called me by name as my school meet's Champion Girl.

I knew all the heart and sacrifice I had committed to my track career, I knew I had earned the distinction, and to hear these people recognize it—to applaud me when I lost a race—lifted my spirits.

POISE

When I had the idea to write a book, I decided on my last chapter first. I knew I wanted to end with a victory lap.

The sport of track and field is unique because it encourages its athletes to take a moment and acknowledge the achievement of conquering a goal that was months and years in the making. It's a graceful gesture.

To me, this book was an opportunity to inspire others, and what's more inspiring than a tale of triumph? My victory lap in London is one of the most vivid memories of my life. I wanted to share that experience with you. All the friends and family who traveled to London were there in the stadium, and as I made my way around, I was able to stop, take photos, and capture the moment with each face. I was able to share the peak of my athletic career with the people who stuck by me and supported me along the way. I was grateful to have individual moments with each of them.

I also dreamed of another. I imagined circling the Olympic Stadium in Rio, an American flag draped over my shoulders, as I celebrated a second gold medal in the 400. I'd take that final lap and walk off into the sunset of legendary retirement. That would be the perfect ending. But we're imperfect people living in an imperfect world. Our only glimpse of perfection comes as we fix our gaze on the perfect Champion, the author and finisher of our faith.

What began at Hayward Field in 2002 with a second-place finish and a celebratory lap was completed there in 2016 with a walk to the finish line. It felt like I was crossing over into my new promised land. It was the beginning—not the end. And I knew this time that defeat had lost its power. That voice calling out to me was the reminder that my Father is watching, and He isn't finished with me yet.

My time on the track was finished, but He was just getting started.

Exactly nine years after my biggest defeat, Ross and I will celebrate our biggest win as we welcome our greatest gift in August 2017.

The desire to win had me running in circles, searching for answers. And, finally, as I chased my self-worth in gold, I ran right smack into grace.

ACKNOWLEDGMENTS

God

I've always felt Your presence and the tugging on my heart to share the good news with others. My first platform was on the track, using my talent and resolve as best I could to inspire. Now You've blessed me with this incredible opportunity to share my message through the pages of *Chasing Grace*. I've prayed throughout this entire process. You're in the name; You're in the cover image; and You're on every page. I couldn't have completed this without the courage I find in You, my heavenly Father.

Family and Loved Ones

Hubby: You are the greatest image of love and humility I have in my life. You teach me every day how to be a better person. You bring out the best in me. Thank you for always being in my corner, for praying with me as we share some of our toughest moments in *Chasing Grace*. I stand tall because you prop me up. I love you . . . always and forever!

Dad: You're always there! It doesn't matter if the call comes at 1:00 a.m. or practice at 9:00 p.m. You're always ready and eager to help me fulfill my passions. No process feels complete without your stamp of approval or your encouraging words. Thanks for your willingness to help me make this book a reality.

Mom: Thanks for reading every page with me, for jogging my memory and providing the supplements that no one else could! You have an ear and a heart that knows no bounds. This book is everything I wanted because of your guidance. I love you!

Shari: Even with your newborn son, you made time to listen to all my chapter ideas and attend my family book review sessions. You always make time for me and make space in your heart for my dreams. I love you and appreciate you more than you know.

Matthew: You're my youngest cousin, yet your wisdom extends far beyond your years. You saw the vision for the book from the very start and challenged me to stick with it, even when it got hard. Your willingness to travel to Austin from Georgetown University, even with your extensive workload, meant everything to me. I see greatness in you; thanks for pulling it out of me.

Tash and Yollie, my two cousins who went above and beyond the call of duty: During holidays together, when we should have been relaxing, you guys read, made edits, and encouraged me to trust my instincts and follow my heart. Thanks for always treating me more like a sister than a cousin.

Rafael & Lahoma: You've both been such a blessing in my life. I appreciate your willingness to jump in when I needed you most to help complete my first book! I'm eternally grateful.

Acknowledgments

Natalie: Our first book is complete! What a blessing it has been to be on this journey with you. From late-night meetings to more texts and phone calls than we'd like to admit, you made this book a reality. You invested your all, re-creating timelines, watching old videos, doing a few of my toughest workouts—you did everything you could to understand me and my message. I couldn't be prouder of our work together. Thanks a million!

My Team: To Carolyn, Tom, Dirk, and the entire Zondervan team, as well as David, Lowell, and Lis at CAA—thank you for believing in me and allowing me to publish my first book! Love you guys so much.

Run with Me

The Story of a U.S. Olympic Champion

Sanya Richards-Ross

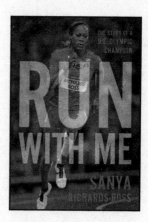

For as long as four-time Olympic gold medalist Sanya Richards-Ross can remember, life has been measured in seconds—the fewer, the better.

The Jamaican-American sprinter has been a star track and field athlete since she first began racing, ranking No. 1 in the world and bringing home Olympic and World Championship accolades. A role model for runners around the world, Sanya's incredible success is matched only by her spirit both on and off the track.

From her early days running in Jamaica to her final race, Sanya shares the importance of determination, courage, and faith. She uses the 4 P's—PUSH, PACE, POSITION, and POISE—a model created by her coach, Clyde Hart, to tackle every obstacle. In her book, Sanya reveals how these strategies have helped her and will help kids learn how to run their best race in life.

Run with Me is Sanya's story—her wins and her losses—chronicling her unique triumphs and trials with fame, family, and faith. Written purposely for the 8-12 audience, this book will inspire kids to pursue their dreams at full speed.

Run with Me has a beautiful embossed cover.

Available in stores and online